Chris Tribble and Glyn Jones

CONCORDANCES
IN THE CLASSROOM

a resource book for teachers

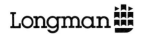

Longman Group UK Limited,
Longman House, Burnt Mill, Harlow,
Essex CM20 2JE, England
and Associated Companies throughout the world.

First published 1990

Set in 10 on 12.5pt Adobe Century Old Style

Printed in Great Britain by Richard Clay plc, Bungay, Suffolk

ISBN 0582 03821 9

Aknowledgements

We would like to thank Tineke van Maanen for sharing her ideas with us and for pointing us towards some of the important background literature, and Paul Mairesse of Eurocentres, Zurich, for the idea which became the WORD macro concordancer given on page 88. Special thanks are also due to Henry Widdowson and Alan Maley for individually agreeing to read and comment on the Concordancing and Literature chapter. Improvements and extensions to this section grew directly from the insights they gave us – weaknesses or limitations in our argument remain our own.

We have used several text handling packages in the writing of this book. Electronic text Corporation of Provo, Utah very generously made it possible for us to use and review WordCruncher, for which we are most grateful. We owe special thanks to Brian Chandler and Longman Dictionaries for use of prototypes of the Longman Mini-Concordancer.

We would finally like to thank Susan Maingay, our publisher, for her encouragement and clear-thinking throughout the project, and Jane Walsh and Steve Crowdy for their patience and commitment in dealing with a manuscript that had to go through the seemingly endless process of transfer from one computerised format to another, and finally to paper.

Chris Tribble and Glyn Jones 1989

Contents

1 *What is Concordancing – what can it do?*

This chapter discusses what concordancing software can do. Part 1 goes briefly into the history of concordancing – both before and after the advent of electronic text processing. Part 2 covers some of the reasons why concordancing is useful to language teachers and language learners.

1 Concordances and concordancers – a short history

In its original sense a concordance is a reference book containing all the words used in a particular text or in the works of a particular author (except, usually, the very common grammatical words such as articles and prepositions), together with a list of the contexts in which each word occurs. Each context may be indicated by means of a precise line reference, or by a short citation, or both.

Books like this have been in use since the Middle Ages, especially in Biblical scholarship. Indeed, they are normally associated with texts which are studied intensively and repeatedly, such as (in the English-speaking world) the Bible and the works of Shakespeare. The simple reason for this is that the labour of compiling a complete concordance for any sizeable text by hand is so colossal that it is worthwhile only if the outcome is expected to be of lasting usefulness. The earliest known complete concordance of the Latin Bible was compiled by the Benedictine Hugo de San Charo in the thirteenth century. Hugo, it is said, was assisted by no fewer than 500 monks.

Computers have changed all this. Provided a text is stored in electronic form, a suitably programmed computer can perform all the tasks involved in compiling a concordance – locating all the occurrences of a particular word and listing the contexts – very rapidly and absolutely reliably. Scholars were not slow to realize this, and so computer programs, called "concordance generators", "concordancers" or, generically, "concordancing software" were developed specially for this purpose.

Thanks to their great speed, computer concordancers have two important advantages over old-fashioned book concordances. Firstly, they can be used interactively. That is, a researcher can quickly obtain a list of contexts for a particular word simply by keying it in on the computer. This means that it is no longer necessary to produce an exhaustive concordance of a text in book form (although this is perfectly possible), as it is much more convenient, and less wasteful of paper, to produce lists for particular words as and when required. Secondly, a computer concordancer will operate on absolutely any written text, however ephemeral, provided it is stored in electronic form (on a floppy disk, for example). As a result, the research techniques made possible by concordances are no longer confined to the study of the Great Books, but are available to all academic disciplines which are concerned with the analysis of text: literary studies, media studies, descriptive linguistics and (the subject of this book) language teaching.

In many instances computer concordancers are used to analyze not individual texts, but large compilations of documents by a particular author or representative of a particular genre, or else writings on a particular topic. Such a compilation of texts is called a corpus (plural corpora).

The most ambitious type of corpus is one that is so big and so varied in composition that it can be considered representative of the language as a whole. There are several such corpora in existence or being compiled, notably in the world of dictionary publishing. These corpora, containing millions of words of English collected from a wide variety of sources, can be analyzed with the aid of a concordancer running on a mainframe computer. The resulting information is invaluable to lexicographers (dictionary writers/ compilers). Conclusions about the meanings and uses of words can be derived from a multiplicity of authentic contexts, and these same contexts can be used as a source of examples for inclusion in the dictionary.

The COBUILD Dictionary project, set up by Birmingham University and Collins publishers, represents the first time that an entire dictionary was based on corpus evidence. It was also instrumental in bringing the potential of concordancing software to the attention of workers in ELT. Tim Johns (1986) was particularly influential in this respect. Hitherto, computer concordancers were programs which ran on expensive mainframe computers in universities. This was not because concordancing is a complex operation (by the standards of computer science it is an extremely simple one), but because the memory storage capacity and the speed of operation required to process large corpora were beyond the reach of small microcomputers. It soon became clear that the techniques used and developed in the course of such large-scale projects could be applied in helping overseas students to learn English, and without the need for the sort of vast corpus required for authoritative lexicographical research.

In any case, in recent years, personal computers have become available with sufficient speed and memory size to make concordancing with quite substantial volumes of text (tens, even hundreds, of thousands of words) a real possibility. Computer concordancers are no longer esoteric research tools. They are becoming, like word processors, a utility which is potentially available to every teacher who has access to a modern personal computer. The purpose of this book is to suggest just some ways in which this new type of utility can help in the teaching and learning of foreign languages.

2 Concordancing today

Concordancing software enables you to discover patterns that exist in natural language by grouping text in such a way that they are clearly visible. These patterns are an important feature of language but the problem has always been that it is extremely difficult to isolate them. The real value of the concordancer lies in this question of visibility. An example of how a concordancer can reveal patterns is given in Figures 1 and 2. Figure 1 contains a short piece of continuous prose. Figure 2 contains a concordance for the definite article *the* for the same text. The concordancer lets you rearrange texts in such a way that it becomes possible to see patterns that would not otherwise be visible.

FIGURE 1

PREPTEXT 1

No more serious phase of the Indian problem has presented itself to the American people than that offered by the Apache tribes. Aided by the desert nature of their country, they have resisted the advances of the whites longer than any other Indian nation. They have fought with bravery and inconceivable cunning. They have committed atrocities that devils alone would seem capable of, and have been subjected to atrocities that devils might blush to commit. They have made their name a terror and a thing of execration to a section of country fi times larger than all New England. They have kept miners for years from treasure deposits that have been regarded as of fabulous richness. They have gained the reputation of being the most treacherous, cruel and inhuman savages that have been known in the United States. People who have been willing to extend sympathy and assistance to the Indians, have stood aghast at the murderous work of the Apaches, and given their opinion that nothing but the extermination of the tribe could ever rid Arizona and New Mexico of a constant liability to outrage and devastation.

(J.P. Dunn *Massacres of the Mountains*, 1886, reprinted Eyre and Spottiswood, 1963)

FIGURE 2

```
        PREPTEXT1    No more serious·phase of the Indian problem has presented itself to the
  the Indian problem has presented itself to the American people than that offered by the A
to the American people than that offered by the Apache tribes.   Aided by the desert nature
hat offered by the Apache tribes.   Aided by the desert nature of their country, they have
nature of their country, they have resisted the advances of the whites longer than any oth
country, they have resisted the advances of the whites longer than any other Indian nation
d as of fabulous richness. They have gained the reputation of being the most treacherous,
s. They have gained the reputation of being the most treacherous, cruel and inhuman savage
and inhuman savages that have been known in the United States. People who have been willin
illing to extend sympathy and assistance to the Indians, have stood aghast at the murderou
stance to the Indians, have stood aghast at the murderous work of the Apaches, and given t
 have stood aghast at the murderous work of the Apaches, and given their opinion that noth
s, and given their opinion that nothing but the extermination of the tribe could ever rid
inion that nothing but the extermination of the tribe could ever rid Arizona and New Mexic
```

The printout in Figure 2 not only reproduces all the instances of the keyword (i.e. the word you ask the concordancer to search for – in this case *the*) in the text, it does so in a way which makes it very easy to see what words occur immediately before and after it in each case. If you cast your eye down the central column it soon becomes apparent that in this text the definite article is often preceded by a preposition, and you may find examples which you can usefully exploit in teaching the use of the definite article in English: *the American people, the whites, the United States.*

A printout like this, with the keyword in a straight column down the middle of the page with as much of the context as will fit running in one line to right and left, is known as a KWIC (keyword in context) concordance. It is the convention used most often by concordancing programs precisely because it facilitates study of the immediate context of the keyword, and it is the convention used in all the examples in this book. However, most concordancers will also let you print out contexts consisting of a complete sentence, or a fixed number of words, or a whole paragraph, or allow you to trace any occurrence back to the original text.

The principle of the KWIC concordance is very simple, then, but it is rich in possibilities. Supposing, for example, you are confronted with one of those questions of detail that occur so often in language teaching, such as "What preposition do you use after *depend*?". Normally you might supply a quick answer, followed by an example which you have thought up on the spur of the moment. With a concordancer in the classroom you can present your students with authentic evidence from which they can work out the answer for themselves, as in Figure 3.

In this case the program has been instructed to find all the instances of words beginning *depend-*, not just in one text but in a corpus of authentic documents

FIGURE 3

```
1 xteen to nineteen-year-old group, depending on whether her birthday falls be
2 d patterns of living which do not depend on fossil fuels at all or depend on
3  depend on fossil fuels at all or depend on them only to a very slight exten
4  begin to get cross or amused. It depends upon their temperament.  <Intervie
5 ange to pay this by direct debit. Depending on when you use it, your Chargec
6  First applications of fertilizer depend on when the turf was laid. If in Sp
```

totalling over 40,000 words. Most concordancers will allow you to implement a search for a part-word like this (a so-called "wildcard" search), so it is very easy to find, for example, all the words ending in *-ing* in a text, or words beginning with *un-*. Similarly, most concordancers will let you search for a phrase like *on behalf of*, or allow you to specify more than one keyword (so that you can search for *far, farther, farthest, further* and *furthest* all at once).

The concordance of a word will often reveal much more than information about the word itself, so the usefulness of concordancing is by no means confined to the study of grammar and lexis. The printout in Figure 4, for example, was obtained in order to examine the way in which certain modal verbs are used to express requests and suggestions in business

FIGURE 4

```
* layer is one of the better ones.  Could you please advise me if the repair i
*  you've sent me over the months.  Could you send a note (or give me a ring)
* ssés Saint-Jacques, Paris 5e. You could also contact Megacentres (the organi
* ontributors, but I don't think we could be joint organisers.  Please let me
* ATEFL. If you prefer, however, we could simply agree to exchange Newsletters
*  print-out (enclosed) so that she could take it with her and talk it through
* d let us know under what terms we could use it in the manner described. We w
* telephone call of this afternoon, could you please repair the videodisc play
*  of setting up the system, and it would be a pity not to take advantage of t
* uitable text for this purpose. We would be grateful therefore if you would 1
* to were not actually enclosed. We would be happy to distribute a questionnai
* er» that we would like to use. We would be interested to know, therefore, if
* Your contributions to Bulletin 12 would be most welcome. I cannot guarantee
* his autumn on your own account we would be very happy to publicise it among
* s, which is a lengthy process!  I would be very interested to have a copy of
* term. If we go along this road we would certainly be interested in collabora
* ould be grateful therefore if you would let us know under what terms we coul
* ro Club members, at least. If you would like contact addresses for these, or
* s for Feb 1989 by parcel post.  I would like to claim the following expenses
* e would be willing to continue. I would like to suggest therefore, that he s
* s of our calendar if possible.  I would like to suggest, therefore, that we
* hange at short notice. However, I would welcome your views on this.  I have
* se it in the manner described. We would, of course, acknowledge the source o
```

correspondence. It was produced by searching for *could* and *would* simultaneously in a corpus of 25 assorted business letters and then sorting the output so that the occurrences of each keyword are grouped together.

In this book we shall be looking at many different applications of concordancing in language teaching. What they all have in common is that they favour learning by discovery. The study of grammar (or vocabulary, or discourse, or style) takes on the character of research, rather than spoon-feeding or rote learning.

In the next chapter we shall consider the practicalities of concordancing by looking at the various types of concordancing software available and describing how to obtain texts and build a corpus. Chapter 3 is about the sorts of linguistic features you can look for and how to implement searches. Chapter 4 discusses ways of using a concordancer to prepare teaching material, and Chapter 5 introduces some ideas for learning activities which can be undertaken with the computer in the classroom and learners at the keyboard. Finally, in Chapter 6, we suggest ways in which concordancing can aid the study of literature.

Chapter summary

- Concordancing was originally a paper-based method of analyzing culturally valuable texts. It provided a list of words and information as to where they occurred in a document.

- Modern concordancing uses a computer to analyze the texts you want to study and lets you display every occurrence of a word in its context.

- Concordancing software is primarily of use in revealing patterns in language which may not otherwise be visible.

- Concordancing software can search for individual words, phrases, parts of words or combinations of words.

2 *Preparation*

In this chapter we explore in more detail the ways in which concordancing can be used in language teaching/learning. Part 1 describes the basic types of software that can be used to create concordances. Part 2 deals with some of the problems you may encounter in putting together collections of machine readable texts that you and your students can use in your own research. Finally, Part 3 gives examples of the ways in which concordancing can reveal information about both native speaker and learner texts.

Section 3 of Chapter 1 gave a general picture of the sorts of things you can search for in texts by using concordancing software. If, however, you are going to use this software effectively it is important to have a clearer idea of exactly what it is that the computer is able to recognize in a text, and how to make the machine look for the things you are interested in. The way you will work will vary from system to system; the fundamental principles are common to all the different concordancers considered in this book.

1 Software

The three main types of concordancing software that are currently available can be divided into:

- those that "read" a text line-by-line and produce concordanced text either to screen, printer or disk as they chunk through the documents you are analyzing (these can be called **streaming concordancers**)

- those that create an index of your text in one (sometimes lengthy) operation and then permit a large variety of text retrieval activities, including concordancing (**text-indexers**)

- those which read the whole text into memory and then proceed to operate on it (**in-memory concordancers**).

The first sort of concordancer is generally not limited to a particular size of text file and is very useful if you are handling files with more than about 50,000 words. The second is very useful if you are dealing with large texts and have fairly sophisticated computing facilities (e.g. an IBM AT compatible and a hard disk). The third type makes possible a very large set of instant-response operations using the minimum of computing facilities, but is limited in the size of texts it can deal with.

a "Streaming Concordancers"

This group has the great advantage of availability. You can buy one of the proprietary text tools currently on the market (see Software Bibliography), write a simple concordancer within a word processor that has macros, or develop one yourself if you have any programming knowledge. There is, however, a drawback. This is speed. Even the fastest of streaming concordancers can take a long time to work through a longish document (10,000 words plus), especially if you are using a standard PC compatible. In a classroom setting it can be difficult to justify locking up the computer in a long concordancing operation if you have other students needing to use the machine. Because of this it is very important to decide carefully on the types of text and the types of search you will do. These must match the software you have to hand.

b "Text-indexing software"

Text-indexing software is still relatively little used. The most appropriate for language teaching/learning purposes is called WordCruncher (see Software Bibliography). This type of software is perhaps ideal for large-scale research – but might prove daunting to those with little computing experience or with limited time or motivation for learning how to use it. Its great advantage is the range of possibilities it offers in retrieving information from texts.

c "In-memory" text consulters

There is a new type of concordancing software which allows for completely different types of text-handling. The only one of which the authors are currently aware is published by Longman as the Longman Mini-Concordancer (see Software Bibliography). This program has the considerable advantage of loading a complete file, or set of files, into the memory of the computer in one operation. The text can then be consulted in a variety of ways, the results obtained being presented to the user more or less instantaneously.

Although the software is limited by the memory size of the computer you are working with and the nature of the PC compatible's disk operating system, with a 512 Kbyte(ram) PC compatible you should be able to handle around 40,000 words of text. If your computer has the maximum memory addressable by MSDOS you should be able to work with up to 50,000 words of text in one operation. For EFL purposes this is a very useful amount of text.

2 Collecting and organizing texts and corpora

No matter how sophisticated your concordancing program may be, the results will only be as interesting as the raw materials on which you put it to work. The raw materials in question are, of course, texts. You may wish to work with an individual text (such as a short story) or else with a corpus made up of several texts.

Individual texts

In literature classes where the objective is to analyze the language of a particular text (a short story, say, or a poem), a copy of that text (in electronic form) is all that you need.

Specialist corpora

On the other hand, in order to investigate the linguistic features that characterize a particular type of text, such as modern short stories in general, or newspaper reports, or advertisements, you need a corpus consisting of several examples of texts of the appropriate type. This is what we mean by a specialist corpus.

General corpora

To study features of the language in general, independently of the styles of particular types of text, you need a general corpus, a collection of texts of as many different types as possible. In this section we are concerned with corpora, both specialist and general.

a The bigger the better?

In practice the size of your corpus is likely to be limited by technical constraints. An in-memory concordancer imposes an absolute restriction on the quantity of text which can be analyzed at one time. With other types of software there may be no fixed maximum, but if your corpus keeps expanding it will reach a size where it takes too long for the program to scan it, or it occupies so many floppy disks as to be unwieldy.

As a general rule, however, the bigger a corpus is the richer and more interesting the output from a concordancing program will be, and the more likely to represent accurately features of the language. The significance of corpus size can most easily be appreciated in relation to the frequency of occurrence of individual lexical items. Take, for instance, a word such as *crime*. Although most native speakers would probably think of this as a "common" word, it actually occurs only about 20 times in every one million words of English. Therefore if one has a small corpus of 50,000 words there ought to be a chance of about one in two that the word *crime* will occur just once. However if the corpus contains just one short text on crime prevention or criminology, it is quite possible that this one text will contribute 20 or 30 occurrences of *crime*, giving a very distorted picture of its distribution in the language as a whole.

This sort of distortion is inevitable with small corpora. However it can be limited by ensuring that the corpus is made up of several short extracts from a wide variety of sources, rather than a few long documents.

Most of the examples in this book were generated using a corpus called the ELT Text Pack (ELTTEXT) consisting of eight sections and totalling about 45,000 words. The corpus contains the following texts:

SECTION 1:   a magazine article about single mothers, written in the first person

SECTION 2:   a short story

SECTION 3:   a short autobiographical article

SECTION 4:   an argumentative article on the theme of industrial production and the environment

SECTION 5:   an article about vegetarianism

SECTION 6:   an extract from the British Highway Code

SECTION 7:   a compilation of transcribed interviews with well-known people

SECTION 8:   a compilation of public information leaflets and advertisements.

Figures 1 and 2 show the effect of a single text within a corpus of this size. In these printouts for *right* one or two texts have been omitted from the corpus in each case. In Figure 1 the Highway Code extract has been left out. In Figure 2 this text has been included, but both of the narrative texts (Sections 2 and 3) have been excluded.

In Figure 1 most of the common meanings and uses of *right* are represented (the opposite of *wrong*, the opposite of *left*, something to which one is entitled, completely, "all right"). In Figure 2 some of these are missing and the meaning "opposite of left" is disproportionately represented. On the other hand the Highway Code extract contributes examples of the very common collocations *turn right* and *right-hand* ... .

One way to proceed is to accumulate several specialist corpora – for example, one of newspaper reports, another of business letters, a third of short stories – to which you add entire documents as you acquire them. You can then build your general corpus by combining extracts from all of these in such a way that you achieve balance and variety while still remaining within whatever limits on overall size you are forced to respect. As your specialist corpora grow, so the texts in your general corpora become more numerous and varied and, if necessary, shorter.

FIGURE 1

```
et7 nths' time. <Diane Abbott:> That's right. <Interviewer:> Are you, um, gettin
et8  turn left, BCP is 1½ miles on the right.   CONDITIONS OF PARKING  Entry to o
et8  , please ask Sister if this is all right. Do not leave food where it can be
et3  e closer to the ground than seemed right. I understood what I had seen in th
et7  hat and I thought, @Oh this is all right!' So after about three or four hour
et2   Bro. Justice knew everything, was right about everything, including the lig
et8  s to Redhill and Crawley A23. Turn Right at next roundabout (A) and join A23
et3  loved me, irresponsibly ('it's all right for him; he doesn't have to look af
et5  to down it with gusto. So it went, right on to the fresh berry tarts, of whi
et7  seventy miles an hour and I landed right on top of him and er as soon as I h
et2  I outJah send the lightning to see right through I". Brother Justice also to
et8  out. At second roundabout (C) turn right to Lowfield Heath and Charlwood. 25
et2  n the aunt stopped questioning his right to his own existence.  At first she
et8  t interest and will exercise their right to vote.  Following the Board's ann
et4  erica, there are many worried men, right up to the White House, calling for
```

FIGURE 2

```
et7 nths' time. <Diane Abbott:> That's right. <Interviewer:> Are you, um, gettin
et6  rough the roundabout. When turning right: Approach in the right-hand lane; k
et8  , please ask Sister if this is all right. Do not leave food where it can be
et7  hat and I thought, @Oh this is all right!' So after about three or four hour
et6   the one to be taken. When turning right: Use the right turn indicator on ap
et6  endant or by remote control and go right across the road. Some also have amb
et8  s to Redhill and Crawley A23. Turn Right at next roundabout (A) and join A23
et6   the side of the road. Take are at right-hand bends. Keep one behind the oth
et6  e amber-coloured studs marking the right-hand edge of the carriageway, red s
et6  ane when you have passed them. The right-hand lane is for overtaking only. I
et6  r than 12 metres, must not use the right-hand lane of a carriageway with thr
et6  hen turning right: Approach in the right-hand lane; keep to that lane in the
et6   emergency (see page 53); . on the right-hand side of the carriageway at nig
et6   there is no footpath, walk on the right-hand side of the road - it is safer
et6  eues and the traffic queue on your right is moving more slowly than you are.
et6   and at night, if you want to turn right it is often safer to stop first on
et5  to down it with gusto. So it went, right on to the fresh berry tarts, of whi
et7  seventy miles an hour and I landed right on top of him and er as soon as I h
et6  away from the kerb. Before turning right or left, moving out to pass or pull
et6  ou overtake, or turn left, or turn right, or slow down, or stop, use your mi
et6  en you intend to overtake, or turn right, or when you have to pass stationar
et8  out. At second roundabout (C) turn right to Lowfield Heath and Charlwood. 25
et8  t interest and will exercise their right to vote.  Following the Board's ann
et6  taken. When turning right: Use the right turn indicator on approach, and mai
et6  ule 55.   170  Overtake only on the right, unless traffic is moving in queues
et4  erica, there are many worried men, right up to the White House, calling for
```

b What should you include in a general corpus?

It follows from the previous paragraph that a general corpus should include as many different types of text as possible. The following guidelines might be useful.

i. As a general rule texts should be authentic. The principal advantage of concordancing is that it gives learners direct access to patterns that exist in natural language. To apply it to texts which have been concocted for the use of learners (in which, therefore, linguistic patterns are artificially controlled) would be to defeat this purpose.

By the same token, learner texts (i.e. homework assignments or essays written by your students) have no place in a general corpus. On the other hand you may wish to compile a separate specialist corpus of learner texts. This can be very useful in two ways: for identifying patterns of error in your students' writing, and for enabling learners to compare their own work with native-speaker texts. We briefly consider the first of these applications in section 3 of this chapter, and we give examples of the second in Chapters 3 and 4.

ii. Use contemporary texts. These can be extracted from journalism of all sorts, novels and short stories (romantic and adventure fiction as well as high-brow literature), advertising and publicity material, public information leaflets, theatre and TV scripts (language written in order to be spoken), textbooks and instruction manuals, and many other sources.

iii. Beware of literature which is old enough to contain archaic linguistic forms or patterns. For English this means that it is safer to exclude anything written more than about 100 years ago.

iv. Beware of dialect. Some (mainly literary) texts contain dialogue which represents non-standard speech in written form, others are written entirely in dialect. Texts like this will yield eccentric spellings and misleading contexts when analyzed with a concordancer.

v. Stick to prose. Verse achieves many of its effects by deliberately violating the normal patterns of the language. For the same reasons it is better to avoid certain way-out or experimental prose works other than in a literature class (see Chapter 6). A concordance analysis of Joyce's *Finnegan's Wake* would no doubt yield fascinating results, but it is not likely to be helpful to the ordinary learner of English!

vi. Include highly technical material only in very small doses. For language learners it is the level of the vocabulary in a text which, more than any other factor, makes it difficult to read. This applies to concordance output just as to any other text. The inclusion of learned articles, scientific reports or any other highly specialized literature will produce contexts in which the vocabulary load is intimidating to all but the most advanced learners. In general a corpus will be more suitable for low-level learners the more texts it contains which have been written for the general reader.

c What about the spoken language?

An ideal general corpus would contain a high proportion of transcribed spoken language. Unfortunately this is not so easy to achieve in practice.

Firstly, transcribing recorded speech is a very tedious and time-consuming process for anyone who is not a trained copy-typist, and this is likely to limit the amount of spoken language you can include.

Secondly, for most types of spoken discourse it is very difficult to obtain recordings in the first place. Interviews and discussions on radio and TV constitute an exception. These are usually unscripted, even if the main points have been rehearsed, but they represent only a small subset of the uses of spoken language. Everyday conversation, on the other hand, is almost impossible to record. Even if participants give their permission, there are few situations in which they will speak naturally and spontaneously in the presence of a microphone. Recording people without their permission constitutes an unjustifiable invasion of privacy.

In general the spoken and written forms of a language are so different that any corpus which contains examples of both has to be balanced in this respect. Just a small amount of transcribed spoken discourse in an otherwise written corpus might yield some very peculiar results.

What follows from this is that you should either make a decision to compile a general written corpus, excluding spoken texts and renouncing any claims to represent or study the spoken language, or make an effort to collect a large sub-corpus of transcribed spoken material. If you choose the latter course, make sure that spoken contexts are easily recognizable as such in the concordancer's output. One way of doing this, more eye-catching than simply tagging them in a certain way, is to transcribe all spoken material in upper-case type.

d Collecting texts

A corpus usually has to be in "plain ASCII format". ASCII (American Standard Information Interchange) refers to the almost universally recognized way of encoding written text in electronic media, with each alphanumeric character uniquely represented by a number; "plain" means that any extraneous information which a word processor may require in order to control layout or typeface has been removed, leaving only the words, punctuation and spacing of the raw text. Most word processors incorporate a facility for converting texts into plain ASCII format.

There are several ways of acquiring plain ASCII text, some more arduous than others. Some of these methods are unsuitable for particular types of text. In practice you will probably find it best to build up a corpus by means of a combination of methods.

i. Keying in

The most tedious and time-consuming way of accumulating text is to type it from scratch by means of a word processor. However for many types of text you will have no alternative.

ii. Scanning

Devices which scan text optically and convert it into ASCII format by OCR (optical character recognition) software are becoming cheaper and more reliable. "Hand-held" scanners are cheaper but more laborious as they have to be rolled across the page in several passes. "Flat-bed" scanners, in which a whole page is inserted at a time as if into a photocopier or FAX machine, are more convenient but much more expensive. With either type of scanner the original text must be of good print quality. In earlier – or less sophisticated – systems the typeface had to conform to one of a limited range of commonly used styles, or the software had to be "taught" every new typeface, character by character. This technology, however, has improved considerably in the last two or three years, and with modern equipment it is possible to achieve very high degrees of accuracy with an entirely acceptable investment of operator time.

Of course, not all texts are amenable to scanning. With spoken dialogue that has to be transcribed from tape, or with handwritten letters, there is as yet no substitute for keying in.

iii. "Read-me" files

Many computer software packages are supplied with ready-made ASCII texts in the form of files, often actually called READDME or READ.ME, which contain the contents of the manual or other instructions to the user. The information is supplied in this form either to save printing costs or because it consists of recent amendments which have not yet been incorporated into the printed manual. It is up to the user to print out the contents of the files on their own printer or simply to view it on screen.

Such files constitute a very restricted genre of text, so unless you wish to study the linguistic features of just this sort of computer literature (in which case it is perfectly justifiable to compile a specific corpus of "read-me" files) they should only be used when mixed in very small doses with other types of text.

iv. Ready-made word-processed documents

In any institution where word processors are used there are bound to be large quantities of text already stored in machine-readable form: correspondence, administrative reports and notices, academic articles and essays, even personal correspondence and creative writing.

Such documents will probably not provide sufficient variety to constitute a general corpus, but they may make a very substantial contribution to one. On the other hand, it may be possible to build up a useful specialist corpus of, say, official correspondence or academic writing, just using internal word-processed documents.

The only disadvantage of using this type of text is that in some cases the contents may be confidential. It may be necessary to spend some time editing to remove some categories of information, or to alter proper names by means of a "search and replace" operation.

v. Electronic communications links

By connecting a modem to your computer (and connecting the modem to a telephone line) you can gain access to unlimited sources of texts, most of which can be "downloaded" (transferred to your computer's memory then saved in ASCII format on floppy or hard disk). These include:

- individual electronic mail contacts, a form of personal correspondence in machine-readable form

- bulletin boards: information services for special interest groups providing news, messages and advertisements

- large-scale public information services like Prestel, which provide up-to-date news in special fields such as finance and sport, as well as current affairs

- document retrieval services which allow the user to download academic articles and other lengthy documents.

All of these cost money. You have to pay for the use of the telephone line, the use of the service (usually an annual or monthly subscription charge), a charge for the time you spend logged on and, often, charges for viewing and downloading particular documents.

vi. Exchange with colleagues

As more and more teachers and researchers start working with concordancers, so it will become easier to make contact with colleagues who have already collected texts and are prepared to swap copies of these with your own. Academic associations and user groups such as MUESLI (see Appendix) may be able to tell you where such informal swap shops already exist, or to put you in touch with like-minded individuals interested in forming one.

vii. Off-the-shelf corpora

Publishers are already responding to the demand for texts by making corpora commercially available in machine-readable form. One such corpus that is available is : the LOB (Lancaster-Oslo-Bergen) Corpus (for details see Appendix).

As a way of acquiring texts this certainly represents the easiest option. Moreover, if you buy a corpus off the shelf there is no reason why you should always use it in the form in which it is supplied. You can manipulate it exactly as you would your own collection of texts, detaching items to supplement your own specialist corpora, or adding new ones to bring the main corpus up to date.

viii. Compiling a learner corpus

In note i on page 18 above we alluded to the possibility of compiling a specialist corpus of learner texts. This should be possible if your students already do some or all of their written assignments on word processors. If this is not the case you can key in learner texts manually.

For some applications your students will be chiefly interested in analyzing their own writing, so a mini-corpus containing work produced by a particular class, or even containing just work written for a particular assignment, will be all that you need.

You can subsequently amalgamate such a mini-corpus with texts from other classes, and so gradually build up a specialist corpus that will enable you to study features of learner writing in general. You will find it useful to tag each piece of work according to the learner's level, first language (if you have multilingual classes) and the nature of the text (composition, essay, commercial letter, etc.).

3 What sort of features can you look for in texts?

Having collected the texts you are going to work with, you must then decide what features you will look for. This will depend on whether you are dealing with native speaker texts or learner texts.

a Native speaker texts

Traditionally, native speaker texts have been the main area for concordance-based research. In Chapter 1 we described how lexicographers have been the people who have used this sort of resource to the greatest extent. To lexicographers the concordance provides invaluable information concerning what actually happens in language use and they manipulate very large quantities of data to produce statistically significant samples.

The grammarian is also able to exploit information from concordances. The Survey of English Usage, the Lancaster-Oslo-Bergen corpus, and COBUILD all provide tremendously important information which not only makes it possible to exemplify grammatical relationships with samples drawn from use, but also to challenge grammatical preconceptions about such things as the nature of prepositions or the way in which future time reference is handled in English. The list below outlines the main types of information you can get from native-speaker text:

- Most common meanings ascribed to particular words
- Most common general contexts for particular words (genre, field)
- Most common immediate collocates (other than fixed phrases and idioms)
- Most common phrase /clump contexts
- The range of vocabulary (type:token ratio) used by particular writers or in particular types of text.

b Learner texts

Concordanced studies of learner texts are a more recent departure. As it has become easier to prepare text for computerized analysis and as more and more students write directly into a computer, the possibilities for concordance studies of "learner language" become correspondingly greater. The Longman/Birkbeck Corpus of Learners' English is one example of the sort of formal study that is being attempted at present, with over a million words of student writing in the first year of collection. This will make it possible to describe some of the ways in which students' first languages influence the way they learn English, what problems students have with certain aspects of English and so on. Even with very small classroom-based studies it is possible to come to some very interesting conclusions about the way students are dealing with English. For the first time the sort of objective study that used to be carried out only in expensively-equipped university departments can be done in most centres for language learning. These studies can begin to deal with topics such as those given below.

Meanings

i.   Most common misuses of words (misunderstandings)

ii. Most common inappropriate uses of words (mistakes of style/register)

iii. Most common lexical errors of particular language groups or levels of learner (source codes identify nationality and level)

Grammar

(All the examples given below are of something having been used incorrectly – it is much harder to get evidence of something *not* being used, for example a student may reformulate a sentence to avoid using a difficult word or structure.)

i.   problems with word order

ii. position of adverbs

iii. prepositions

iv. misuse of tense

v.   misuse of affixes

vi. contexts in which articles are misused

This is a very small set of examples, but it does give an idea of the ways in which concordancing can reveal problem areas when it is used on student writing. There are difficulties, of course. The main one has already been mentioned – you cannot search directly for something that has not been used.

Conclusion

Concordancing gives you a way of seeing patterns in language in use that would remain hidden under other circumstances. Once you have chosen or prepared the software you want to use and have put together a body of texts for study, you have access to a uniquely powerful way of studying language. The remaining chapters in this book look at ways in which you can turn this research tool into a practical aid for teaching/learning.

Chapter summary

■ There are various types of software available – these can be categorized as "streaming", "indexing", and "in-memory" concordancers.

■ Large, general corpora are best for information about particular lexicai items, small corpora can give useful information about grammar words and specific types of written or spoken language.

■ Native speaker texts provide authentic examples of language in use.

■ You can find out about problems that students have with the meanings of words and the way they use words when you study learner texts.

3 *Searching*

This chapter discusses specific ways of using concordancing software to find information in texts. Part 1 deals with the use of wordlists and frequency tables that you can produce with the software. Part 2 discusses the problem of establishing what a word is for computing purposes and explains the use of wildcards. Part 3 gives a detailed listing of the particular patterns you can search for. Part 4 describes how concordances can be labelled to show their original source and Part 5 discusses how concordances can be displayed so as to reveal particular types of information.

In the two previous chapters we have looked in general terms at what concordancers are, what they can do, and the sorts of text you can study with them. This chapter describes some basic techniques you can use to find particular types of information in the texts you are studying. Different concordancing software packages use different conventions to achieve their ends, but there are some basic principals that are common to most. Once you have mastered these, it is possible to use your concordancer to get just as much or as little information as you want. This is important, for once you have started to use any form of electronic text retrieval system you will discover that often your biggest problem is not too little but too much information.

1 Wordlists and frequency tables

Before using your text-handling program to create a concordance, it is worth remembering that the software can provide other extremely useful information in the form of wordlists. With most text concordancers it is possible to create a table that lists not only all the words that occur in a text, but also gives their frequency of occurrence. You often have the option of setting cut-offs for maximum and minimum frequencies so that you are not overwhelmed by the numerous occurrences of *the* or *of*, or by the 30% or 40% of words that only occur once in the text. By creating a frequency table before running a concordance across a text it is possible to have a much better idea of which items it will be fruitful to select. It saves a great deal of guesswork at the beginning of a concordancing session if you make it a habit to begin with wordlists and then move on to analysis.

2 Words and wildcards

| **a** Words

When concordancing software (or any other program) is looking for something in a text file it is important to realize that the machine is not looking for something that we recognize as a "word". It has no way of dealing with such a concept. The computer is simply looking for a "string" of characters that are stored on electronic media as numerical code. This code gives a specific number to every letter of the alphabet as well as numbers allocated to punctuation marks, some graphics characters and also blank spaces. This is important. If, for example, you are working with a word processor and you try to look for the word *new*, not only will you find that *newly, newest* and *newcomer* are presented as instances of the word you are looking for, you will also come up against *newt, knew, Newton* and *Agnew*. You will also find that if you try to get round this problem by looking for *new*, (where you specify a blank space on each side of the word as a search string) you will fail to find perfectly good examples of the word where it arises in the same setting as a punctuation mark – *new,* is not the same string as *new* so far as the computer is concerned, even if it is the same word to a human reader.

If we bear this in mind, it becomes clear that looking for a word in a text might not be so easy as it might appear at first sight. Fortunately, text-handling software gets round some of these problems by building in definitions such as the following: "A word is any character string that is bounded either by blank spaces or a set of specified punctuation marks." In this way it is possible to give an instruction to look for *new* and indeed be presented with only that word irrespective of how many other instances the combination of letters *n, e, w* might occur in the text and irrespective of the punctuation marks that *new* might have attached to it.

| **b** Wildcards

If you want to look for *new* and also find other forms associated with this word such as *newly, newness*, and *news*, you have to have software which allows for the use of wildcard operators. In the same way as the Disk Operating System (DOS) uses wildcards to speed up file handling (e.g. the DIR command lets you look for all files by typing *.*), most text-handling software also exploits such features. Wildcards are symbols that have an "open" meaning and, by building them into the concordancing software, designers are able to exploit the computer's capacity to let one symbol stand for one or many other things. The two basic conventions that most text-handling software works with are the asterisk * which can mean "any string of characters" and the "at" sign @ or question mark ? which can be used to mean "any single character". In this way it is possible to look for any present participle by searching for *ing*. This, of course, throws up plenty of words that are not present participles (e.g. *sing, thing*). However, as you can then eliminate the unwanted words in a word processor – or exclude many of them before you begin to search by asking only for words of five or more letters, it is still a very powerful facility.

3 Possible search patterns

This section gives a brief summary of the specific sorts of item you can look for in a text. The list is reasonably extensive and covers the main search potential of most of the more sophisticated concordancing programs. Other programs may well be more limited in their scope, but their accompanying manuals will give you full instructions on exactly what they can do.

a Punctuation

The smallest units that the concordancer can look for are punctuation marks. This is, in fact, extremely helpful. If you are interested, for example, in theme/ rheme patterns in certain texts, a concordance on full stops gives you valuable information about the ways in which the sentences in the text you are studying begin and end:

FIGURE 1

```
have lost important years of my adolescence. I know that I have gained treme
ad it and see what others have gone through. I like to think I've been helpful t
     manhood by a terrible mistake I had made. I love my unborn baby deeply, just a
      t every- thing that had happened to them. I really enjoyed our conversations and
       s book will contribute to providing this. I think it's good to have a book on te
      ey're taking on if they do have the baby. I wouldn't wish it upon anybody to get
       e a variety of teenage mothers as I could. I  wrote in several magazines asking
          thing. I don't think of myself like that. I'm lucky it's worked out quite differ
            it is totally  changed by having a baby. If girls are under sixteen, they can e
```

b Single words

The most common category you will look for with a full-function concordancer is the complete word. This can be of any length and contain any "legal" characters – that is, characters that the software can recognize. Figure 2 shows an example of this.

FIGURE 2

```
urrent rates of use; and, far from being interested in studying the possibilities of alter
arted to talk about myself and he wasn't interested in  that too, so I changed the topic t
. it could be a  business man and so more interested in culture. To this  bussines man I wo
and  places where we might be related or interested in.  After having seen the city and ha
n  which he might have been connected or interested, I would take  him away from the city,
```

c Verb forms

It is also possible to group all the forms of a verb under a single "headword" so that, for example, all the occasions when *go* is used in a text or text corpus (i.e. *go, goes, going, gone, went*) can be collected together for study (see Figure 3).

27

FIGURE 3

```
dwill of Spain; he was willing to go great lengths in humouring the Spanish
ve agreed that the emperor should go on an expedition for the conquest or d
in after days was ever willing to go.  When Charles came to the throne the
  horse if he could persuade it to go. Finally, they agreed to his taking, a
d make the population hesitate in going to extremes. He 1934, admitted, how
ons of the two provinces, but was going to lend a hand to the exclusion of
er the new Ukrainian Republic was going to last very long, in which case cu
bourne did indeed make very heavy going. It sailed from Woolwich on 7 Decem
any one he could, to keep his men going; and when money was forthcoming, he
m, while Sicily, which had always gone with Naples, was given to the duke o
aid to German expansion'.s Having gone far beyond the minutiae of the east
e of six galleys, with which they went on a predatory expedition to the Lev
arranged with Lord Buckhurst, who went out as ambassador during Leicester's
munition for the milita which all went out together in the GreaT Easrern at
consisting of thirty vessels, and went on his way ravaging the coasts and i
```

d Word families

Similarly, it is possible with much concordancing software to group together words that are semantically related – either as semantic sets where *sister, mother, daughter, aunt, niece, mummy, grandmother* could come under the headword *Female*, or co-hyponyms such as *sheep, pig, cow*, could be collected under the superordinate *Domesticated animal*. This would involve setting the search command on your concordancer so that all the words you wished to study would be found in a single search and then saving and printing these words in a single, probably alphabetically sorted, concordance.

e Any word/ part-word + specific affix

The next category involves the use of wildcards in order to deal with word morphology. It is possible to use the * to specify word endings (Figure 4) or word beginnings and endings (Figure 5) and in this way, if you have appropriate data to work on, you can provide examples of the different forms that words can take as well as the contexts in which they occur.

FIGURE 4

```
r Chargecard can give you up to 8 weeks' interest-free credit. And if you choose to settle
ant in terms of his Liberalism - no more interesting or valuable to the historian tha as w
t daily; we believe it to be in Members' interests that Abbey National has the freedom to
```

FIGURE 5

```
                    *terest*        [eg. disinterested, uninteresting]

f with the two powers who had been been; bitterest enemies she broke up the European syste
umstances that she could afford to be so disinterested in continental affairs: having no i
ld not even excuse his incapacity by the disinterestedness of his motives. The only compre
donment by Russia of her traditional, if self-interested, patronage of the Bulgarians; nor
```

f A set number of any characters + specific beginning/ending

The single character wildcard (conventionally ? or @) makes it possible to search for words of specific lengths with or without prescribed affixes.

Such wildcard combinations could also be used for example in searches for four-letter words beginning in *s* and ending in *k*, where a code like "s??k" could be used.

FIGURE 6

```
    ??????ed [eg. invested, deprived, collated]

Prince Schwarzenburg. Aberdeen's tactic achieved nothing: when he did write to Schwarzenb
and uncle's life that he both loved and despised - would be lost to him forever and he to
a part of nature but as an outside force destined to dominate and conquer it. He even talk
rer the time of the vote, we will send a detailed document to each Member setting out our
re is no security for anyone...'  He now returned to Englad as fast as travel in February
```

g Phrase of "n" words

The concordancer is not limited to searches for single words. As a search string is simply a continuous set of characters, and as a blank space is considered to be a character by the computer, a search string such as *while this is* is as easy to find as the search string *a*. It is just a collection of codes. This makes searches for idioms and fixed collocations both simple and powerful.

FIGURE 7

```
                interest in

TALIAN UNIFICATION: JULY  I  Gladstone's interest in Italy long pre-dated his famed Letter
ure Europe.  I am very happy to see your interest in our culture and way of  life. You wil
```

h Word/phrase + word/phrase separated by an arbitrary number of intervening words

More sophisticated concordancers are not only able to look for phrases, some of them can also carry out what are called "collocation" or "proximity" searches. Here you are looking for a combination of words that coexist in the same context but which are not necessarily contiguous. This might be a collocation pattern such as *pretty tired/well/uncomfortable* etc; or a combination important in discourse organising such as *it ... that* or *there ... (is/are/ were/being/be/been) etc.* In either case you cannot predict how many intervening words there will be between one element in your search string and another. You can, however, set the maximum number of intervening words for the combination in which you are interested and then carry out the search.

FIGURE 8

```
      it ....... that          [eg. it is important that, it seems that, it has been said tha
ESSAY      70  estrict local and regional autonomy it could be demonstrated that local auto
DISSERA   189  ops of the loading cycle in detail, it can be seen that :-  i For each eleme
DISSERA   242  hich will be stated later. However, it has been shown that some of the metho
ESSAY     417  eave the economy on its own and let it adjust towards equilibrium. They beli
ESSAY     305  e important than any other policies it is that its primary objective is the
ESSAY     432  re the arguments for privatisation? It is also believed that privatisation c
ESSAY     323  er to follow  academic fields since it is generally believed that whatever
ESSAY      37  ueous solution. In addition to this it is reported by former investigators t
DISSERA   224  presented in Figure 5.9.1 to 5.9.3. It is clearly seen that there is a good
```

4 Showing where your information comes from

It is often very important to be able to show the sources of your concordance examples. If you are working with a variety of text samples and want to deal with them comparatively you must be able to mark each line's source. Concordancing software can usually provide a user with ways of marking the output from searches by using source labels. One widely used system is COCOA (named after one of the early general purpose concordancing programs). In a COCOA reference the user can specify a category and a reference in a code that is typed at the beginning of a specific document thus:

```
<T PARLIAMENT AND FOREIGN AFFAIRS>
<A TURNER J A>
<J EHR1900>
<D 4.00>

IT may be of interest at the present time to study in
detail the long-continued attempts once made in behalf
of parliament to ..........
```

Here the opening and closing angle brackets, < >, contain a category label, "J" (standing for JOURNAL), and this is followed by a specific reference that will be used in the final output. If the concordance contains examples from various years of the journal in question this information can then be displayed beside each concordance line in this way:

```
                              finally      7


EHR1919 dicious economy of her favours. She finally confirmed her power over him by a
EHR1919 715 and 26 May 1716; and these were finally confirmed by the treaty of Madrid
EHR1900 ance became more menacing. But when finally the nation was stired, and a new
EHR1930 engagement. The Germans did in fact finally refuse to march without a guarant
EHR1930 e not recovered rapidly enough. And finally, additional troops were taken ove
EHR1930 d the treasurer-at-war's  money and finally ruined Buckhurst's scheme for its
EHR1988  south of Russia a nationality will finally grow up entirely separate from th
```

In this way it is possible to trace the use of a particular word in each of the texts being studied.

Other types of software will ask you to type in a simple label between (perhaps angle brackets) or will exploit DOS file names as a way of telling you from which file each line of the concordance printout has been taken.

5 Display

It is not only possible to select the word or combination of words you want the concordancing software to search for, it is also possible to specify the form in which the target string will be displayed. The implications of this become clear when you compare the following examples.

a Concordances
– unsorted

We have already seen unsorted concordances where the word and its context are given in the same order as they occur in the text. This gives us an example such as Figure 9, where the line reference numbers show that each occurrence of the target word is printed as it arises in the text. An unsorted concordance can be useful as a way of demonstrating change in the use of a word across a complete text (for example when working on a literary text – see Chapter 6 Section 3) but is not particularly illuminating if you are trying to discover any grammatical or collocational relationships associated with the target word.

FIGURE 9

```
Unsorted                                        world    11

 46 .es for they were located in another world, occupied different space, transcende
 49 .eing he knew who also moved in this world, and Bro. Justice he could never tran
 52 .and accepting the mysteries of this world. At first his father and mother somet
 56 .am up and down in a fluid. And this world was so satisfying that after a time e
 67 .e knew instinctively that if in the world he had nothing else, he was still ric
134 . as if he had been plucked from one world which was small and snug and mis- tak
155 . ones ever seen in that part of the world were ones who would simply be passing
192 .oy alone had been able to enter his world, questioning only its superficial man
194 . ask for or take anything from this world. The boy simply was. He was also angr
296 .- Bro. Justice, the room, the magic world, even the order of the aunt and uncle
307 .uld reach through to the mysterious world he felt certain existed beyond. He wa
```

b Concordances – left context / right context sorted

Alphabetically sorted concordances are able to show things very differently. If you consider the two examples for *world* shown in Figure 10 it is possible to see very clearly from the left sort that *world* is a word that accepts various determiners and that the definite article is dropped when other determiners are employed.

The right sorted concordance gives very little grammatical or "vocabulary use" information in this case, but if you take another word such as *aunt* in Figure 11, not only is it easy to discover the class of verbs that are associated with this grammatical subject/actor, but it is also possible to see how the characterization of this particular person in the story is established through the nearly exclusive use of a set of verbs concerned with mental states and attitudes. In short samples such as these the patterning is less transparent than in longer examples where left/right sorting suddenly lays bare structures that are present in the writing but very difficult to spot with the unaided eye.

c Larger contexts

While a single line the same size as a computer screen (usually 79 characters long) can sometimes give enough information about the word that has been concordanced, it is often useful to display more. One way to do this is to use a condensed typeface on your printer and then you can specify a line 135 characters long. In addition, it is possible to take a much longer context and display each example as continuous text (as a sentence of a paragraph if you wish). This, however, loses much of the advantage of the single line entry, for now things cannot be seen so easily.

FIGURE 10

```
Right Sorted                         world

being he knew who also moved in this world, and Bro. Justice he could never transform
 and accepting the mysteries of this world. At first his father and mother sometimes
 - Bro. Justice, the room, the magic world, even the order of the aunt and uncle's li
ould reach through to the mysterious world he felt certain existed beyond. He was so
he knew instinctively that if in the world he had nothing else, he was still rich bec
ces for they were located in another world, occupied different space, transcended dim
boy alone had been able to enter his world, questioning only its superficial manifest
t ask for or take anything from this world. The boy simply was. He was also angry at
wam up and down in a fluid. And this world was so satisfying that after a time even w
y ones ever seen in that part of the world were ones who would simply be passing thro


Left Sorted                          world

ces for they were located in another world, occupied different space, transcended dim
 - Bro. Justice, the room, the magic world, even the order of the aunt and uncle's li
ould reach through to the mysterious world he felt certain existed beyond. He was so
, as if he had been plucked from one world which was small and snug and mis- takenly
he knew instinctively that if in the world he had nothing else, he was still rich bec
y ones ever seen in that part of the world were ones who would simply be passing thro
wam up and down in a fluid. And this world was so satisfying that after a time even w
t ask for or take anything from this world. The boy simply was. He was also angry at
being he knew who also moved in this world, and Bro. Justice he could never transform
 and accepting the mysteries of this world. At first his father and mother sometimes
```

FIGURE 11

```
149 T. the Pen before he, according to the aunt, began to turn queer' with his beard
143 T. Bro. Justice was double- edged. The aunt both feared Bro. Justice and grudgingl
242 T. e unbelievable step of going to the aunt herself to plead with her please look
244 T.  look after the little boy. But the aunt, immensely pleased that Bro. Justice h
167 T. ical appearance, the thing that the aunt noticed and disliked most about Bro. J
137 T. ect fit. And in an unspoken way the aunt seemed to criticise him for his failur
176 T. lf into his new life, that even the aunt stopped questioning his right to his o
  7 T. ncle called the living room and the aunt the parlour, and on the far side this
185 T. t the Rastafarian. Now, just as the aunt thought, Bro. Justice was angry about
 15 T. e house was painted green since the aunt thought it was a restful colour for th
214 T. ing after the chickens, helping the aunt with her vegetable garden. He could no
```

Chapter summary

■ Using the concordancer to create wordlists and frequency tables is often the best way to start to study a text or texts.

■ You can use wildcards to make your searches more specific and effective.

■ Many concordancers allow you to display the source for each line of a concordance alongside the context.

■ The way in which you sort the lines of a concordance can have a very important influence on the amount of information the concordance will give you.

4 *Concordance output as teaching material*

This chapter is about ways in which the output from a concordancer can be turned into material which can be used in the language class. Several examples are given of exercises, worksheets and lessons produced with the aid of a concordancing program.

1 The printed output

In Chapter 2 we saw how to use a concordancer to obtain all sorts of linguistic information, and we saw several examples of the resulting output. We now turn to ways of using this output to create language-learning activities.

In this chapter we shall deal with written teaching materials based on concordance output. We assume that you, the teacher, have access to a PC, a concordance program and a printer and that you can use these to prepare worksheets for your students. In the next chapter we shall explore the additional potential of giving students direct access to the concordancer.

The possible applications of concordance output are much too diverse to list exhaustively. Here we just give some examples of exercise types. These should be treated as models which you can adapt to your own needs, as starting points for your own experiments.

In any case, as we saw in Chapter 2, the quality of the output of any concordance depends very much on the content of the corpus on which it is run. If you try to reproduce our example exercises using a different corpus you could be disappointed, as your corpus might fail to produce suitable data. On the other hand, it might yield quite different insights and possibilities. The best approach is to study the output with an open mind before deciding how to exploit it. If it turns out to be unsuitable for the exercise which you had planned, perhaps other uses will occur to you.

Two generalizations can be made about applications of concordance output, in spite of their diversity. Firstly, most of them favour discovery learning. That is, they present language in a way that enables learners to discover new knowledge for themselves, rather than being spoon-fed. Secondly, they do this by providing examples of authentic language. The fact that the source material for exercises is drawn from real life rather than concocted by teachers increases motivation, as it gives learners immediate contact with the target language in use.

Some of the activities described below could be realized by taking the raw printout into class and simply talking through it, explaining what you want your students to do. But you inevitably achieve a more effective presentation if you edit the output in some way, if only by adding a heading at the top and some questions at the bottom. In general the most convenient way to do this is by using a word processor. Generate output in the form of an ASCII file, if your concordance program will allow you to do this, and then load this into your word processor. When you have done whatever editing is necessary you can print out a master copy of the completed exercise, from which you can run off photocopies for your students.

However, if your concordancer will only produce paper output, or if you do not have a word processor or are not used to using one, most of the exercises we describe can be produced with the aid of more old fashioned text-editing facilities – scissors, paste and correcting fluid.

No matter how smartly produced your exercises are, your students will find them confusing at first. A KWIC printout looks very strange to someone who has not seen one before, and learners are not likely to appreciate the reasons for using this type of material until you explain the background. Before you give your students concordance-based exercises for the first time, conduct a brief introductory session. Explain what a concordance is, show them some example printouts and let them see the program in action, if possible. Tell them how your corpus is made up and get them to discuss the advantages and disadvantages of using a computer to find lists of examples in authentic texts.

2 Activity types

a Deducing the meaning of the keyword

Perhaps the most obvious use of concordance output is to ask learners to supply the meaning of the keyword. The ability to deduce the meaning of unfamiliar words by means of contextual clues is a great asset in language learning. It enables learners to cope with texts which would otherwise prove far too difficult, and to expand their vocabulary in the process. Teachers frequently, and rightly, exhort learners to "work it out from the context" when they encounter new vocabulary, rather than relying completely on the dictionary.

Unfortunately, this is not always possible. The context in which a new word is found does not necessarily contain sufficient information for even a native speaker to deduce its meaning. Concordance output, however, by presenting several contexts of the same word simultaneously, greatly increases the chances of success, while making the process of deduction an intriguing problem-solving task. Consider Figure 1, where the keyword has been replaced by a nonsense word. The first line gives little indication of the meaning of "speg", beyond the syntactic information that it is a noun. Much the same is true of most of the other contexts, taken in isolation. In conjunction with each other, however, they enable one to narrow down the range of possible meanings to "some sort of food or drink", and then finally to the original word (*milk*).

FIGURE 1

```
* ntary benefit, maternity grant and speg and vitamin tokens. (This has recent
* relatively cheap, on tides of free speg and orange juice, but good cloth in
* nimals give us painlessly, such as speg and eggs.  The proposition that meat
*  consisting in large part of eggs, speg, cheese or other speg products is hi
* art of eggs, speg, cheese or other speg products is high in protein. Lentils
* ee a bus stopped, or near a parked speg float or mobile shop. Watch out for
```

However, there is no guarantee that a concordance of a particular word will produce contexts that contain adequate clues as to meaning. Moreover, the words which learners (especially advanced learners) do not know are likely to be the less frequent ones. These are likely to appear only a very few times, if at all, in the corpus. It is essential, therefore, to examine a printout carefully in order to decide whether your learners will be able to deduce meaning from the information that it gives. In your mind try replacing the keyword with a nonsense word and put yourself in the learner's position. Could you work out the meaning of this strange word from the contexts given?

Vocabulary study is not only a matter of learning the meanings of new words. Even if a particular concordance does not enable you to pinpoint meaning it is likely to reveal all sorts of other information about the keyword: grammatical features, common collocations, different meanings, idiomatic and metaphorical uses, stylistic features, connotations. The next three exercise-types are directed towards these aspects of vocabulary.

b Grammatical features

Many of the grammatical features of a word are immediately apparent from its context, for example, whether a verb or adjective is followed by a particular preposition (see Figure 2) or the position which a particular adverb usually occupies in the sentence (see Examples of applications A Chapter 5).

FIGURE 2   **A** What preposition is used after *interested*? Do these examples tell you anything else about the way in which we use this word? (Look at number 1).

B What preposition is used after *depend*? What sort of word often comes after the preposition?

```
1 tes of use; and, far from being interested in studying the possibilities of
2 e-cream van - children are more interested in ice-cream than in traffic.  60
3 iane, when did you first become interested in politics? <Diane Abbott:> I'v
4 Diane Abbott:> I've always been interested in politics, as um, far back as I
5 mbridge, and umm I'm still very interested. I'm just doing a series of progr
6 iewer:> One ... one thing which interested me was. um, polite violence, like
```

```
* xteen to nineteen-year-old group, depending on whether her birthday falls be
* d patterns of living which do not depend on fossil fuels at all or depend on
*  depend on fossil fuels at all or depend on them only to a very slight exten
*  begin to get cross or amused. It depends upon their temperament.  <Intervie
* ange to pay this by direct debit. Depending on when you use it, your Chargec
*  First applications of fertilizer depend on when the turf was laid. If in Sp
```

It is often possible to study grammatical features of the language in general (not merely features of particular words) via the concordances of groups of associated words or phrases. Figure 3 shows an extended worksheet intended as a vehicle for teaching the grammar of Reported Speech at Intermediate level. It is based on unedited concordances for *said* and *told*. The suggested procedure for using the worksheet is as follows:

Stage A: Explain what is meant by Reported Speech, giving a few examples. If appropriate (i.e. with a monolingual class) ask students to give examples in their own language.

Stage B: Hand out the worksheet (Figure 3). Ask the students to work through as far as Question 4 individually, then to discuss their findings briefly in small groups.

Stage C: Ask groups to report back to the class. They should be able to tell you that according to the evidence *told* is always used with an indirect object, whereas *said* is never used with one, and that in the apparently anomalous number 13 the indirect object does not appear after *told* as this is in the passive voice.

Stage D: Repeat the procedure for the remaining questions to see if the students are able to work out at least some of the rules governing verb tenses in Reported Speech.

FIGURE 3 In the following concordances the verbs *said* and *told* are always used to introduce Reported Speech. Read the examples and answer the questions below.

```
1  age of eight what she'd done: she said she'd worked in an office, done cler
2 offered me a race, you see, and we said that ... 'cos he was having a bit of
3 t. I answered my own question, and said that I thought we must be middle cla
4 shiny instrument". Brother Justice said that that was why he had no mirror i
5 his reading of the Bible.  The boy said the old man had taken to spending a
6 t through I". Brother Justice also told him that he would be safe from light
7 o Bro. Justice. Besides, something told him that if he once deserted, then e
8 elephant carved in ivory. The man told him to always turn the elephant to f
9 dies'. When I was about twelve she told me how she'd 'flung' a sixpenny piec
10 ed with newspapers. She must have told me once that I was lucky to have a w
11 my grandmother, and she, puzzled, told me that Edna had never worked in any
12 ounding silence. Later, my mother told me they had to lip read: they couldn
13 visited my primary school) she was told that I'd be going into the eleven-pl
14 is sort of thing and umm so when I told them their reaction was much differe
15 er frequently reminded me) and who told you to accept the impossible contrad
```

1. What sort of word nearly always comes immediately after *told*?

    ....

2. Compare the examples of *said* (numbers 1 – 6). Can you write a rule to determine when you use *said* and when you use *told* to introduce Reported Speech?

    ....

3. Number 13 seems to be an exception. Can you explain why?

    ....

4. Now make a note of the main verb which follows *said* or *told* in the left-hand column in the table overleaf. The first three have been entered for you.

	Verb	Original words
1.	had worked	"I've worked in an office ... "
2.	? ?	? ?
3.	thought	"I think we must be ... "
4.		
5.		
6.		
7.		
8.		
9.		
10.		
11.		
12.		
13.		
14.		
15.		

5. Look at the examples again and try to work out what each speaker actually said (in Direct Speech). Write down what you think the speaker's exact words were in the right-hand column in the table above. The first three have been entered for you. Number 2 shows that you cannot always guess what the speaker said as the concordance does not give you enough information.

6. In the places where you have written something in the right-hand column, look at the main verb. What tense is it in? Compare it with the verb in Reported Speech (in the left-hand column. You should find that the tense of the verb has changed in every case. Can you write any rules about how verb tenses change in Reported Speech?

Whether or not a grammar point is amenable to study in this way depends on whether it is associated with lexical items which are easy to search for. This, in turn, depends on the language that you are studying. In German, for example, the formation and use of the passive voice can easily be studied via a concordance of the various forms of the verb *werden*. The same cannot be done in English because the auxiliary verb used to form the passive voice, *be*, has so many other uses. In French particular verb forms such as the subjunctive mood can be studied by a wildcard search for their highly

characteristic endings. In English it should be possible to track down the comparison of adjectives via the concordance of *than* (see Figure 4), or the formation of conditional sentences by searching for *if*.

As with word meanings, there is no guarantee that a concordance intended to illustrate a point of grammar will produce the information expected or desired. There may simply be no examples of the target structure, or of a particular aspect of it, in the corpus. On the other hand, a concordance will frequently reveal additional information that can be both illuminating and surprising. The concordance of *than* in Figure 4, for example, is not very useful for demonstrating the "long adjective" rule as it contains only one instance of an adjective preceded by *more*. It does, however, contain plenty of examples of the comparison of adverbs, often neglected in course books, and of *rather than*, as well as the common idiomatic uses *...than ever*, *...than you think*, and the structure *better to* (verb) *than to* (verb).

FIGURE 4

```
* pstick. She looked so much  better than the fat, spreading South London moth
*  safe rule is never  to get closer than the overall stopping distance shown
* pping at Marks & Spencer is easier than ever, with a Chargecard.  When you'r
* peed; you may be going much faster than you think. Do not  speed up to get a
* ditions. Your speed will be higher than you  think - 50 mph may feel like 30
* on of peace obviously looms larger than ever before in  human history. And h
* ng involved an in-  crease of less than 5,000 million tons of coal equivalen
* ibute (reckoned in  calories) less than four per cent to the world total. In
* drawing a trailer, or a bus longer than 12 metres, must not  use the right-h
* after conversion from holding more than 15% of the  shares in the successor
* ookshop of their choice  from more than 3,000 throughout the UK and Ireland.
* e Board?   A  W will do much more than that. We will hold meetings with Mem
* ers stay down at any time for more than three minutes  without a train arriv
* ervation at  intervals of not more than two miles and they apply to all lane
* atch in fascination as  more often than not he missed his mouth and the carr
* coming up behind much more quickly than  you think. Make sure that the lane
* enticeship - I deduce that, rather than  know it - sometime, it must have be
* ith him for most of the day rather than several visitors all at once,   which
* heelers are much less  easy to see than larger vehicles and that their rider
* offer the customer  better service than our competitors.  We believe that on
* take the bend a little bit sharper than him; so I took off,  was going towar
* n your right is moving more slowly than you are. Never move  to a lane on yo
*  that, um something which is worse than in other  countries, or ...    <Dian
* , especially when you are younger than usual. So I like  to think I'm helpi
```

c Homonyms and synonyms

Because a concordance program searches for particular combinations of letters, and not for words as such, any homonyms that are in the corpus will appear indiscriminately in the same printout. For example, if you search for *lead*, intending to investigate the use of the verb (*lead-led-led*), the output will also contain instances of the related noun (*Dogs must be kept on a lead*), as well as references to the metal (Pb). This often comes as a surprise; we are so used to thinking of the words in question as completely distinct items that it is easy to forget that they are homonyms. However, you can turn this to advantage by simply asking your learners to separate the different meanings.

Figure 5 shows an exercise based on a concordance of *like*. The objective is to give learners, of Lower Intermediate level or above practice in identifying parts of speech in context.

FIGURE 5   In which of the contexts below is *like* a verb (as in *I like chocolate*), and in which contexts is it a preposition (as in *My brother eats like a horse*)?

```
 1  00'. If we are now using something like  7,000 million tons of coal equivale
 2  away from their homes, and treated like  outcasts.    So don't break up a fr
 3  nable to make it. I wanted to walk like  that, a short skirt, high heels, br
 4  n you are younger than usual. So I like   to think I'm helping somebody else.
 5   than you  think - 50 mph may feel like 30 mph - so be sure to use your spee
 6  e desk. It was a damp mouldy smell like a  dirty wet dog or a saddlecloth ca
 7  ther, the boy imagined that he was like a space traveller in  baggy clothes
 8  enly placed into another which was like a suit many times  too large and to
 9  ils  xylophone, marimba - which is like a xylophone except lower in pitch -
10  ld or visit as often as they would like because they work or have other  chi
11  tical principles into  practice, I like meeting people, and I'm pleased to b
12   There are increasing numbers who, like myself, are for one reason  or anoth
13  know about Stravinsky or something like that  then they're quite lost.    <I
14  verything. I don't think of myself like that. I'm  lucky it's worked out qui
15  lodger's room  already occupied. I like the idea of being the daughter of a
16  et for another  reason: he did not like the old man. In fact he feared and
17  n my case I can sleep as long as I like the rest of the time.    <File Seven
18  book. Testing hundreds (it  seemed like thousands) of recipes in my own kitc
19  Young people are often curious and like to experiment with the latest  craze
20  cial  offer for everyone. If you'd like to find out more about Holidays in
21   lies in the  people we employ. We like to make our branches friendly and we
22   what others have gone  through. I like to think I've been helpful to somebo
23  call kitchen  sink things which is like woodblocks and castanets and gurious
```

VERB: ....

PREPOSITION: ....

The same principle can be applied to distinguishing between different meanings of the same word, or identifying the precise differences in meaning between words that are almost synonymous. The exercise in Figure 6 includes both of these activities, using a combined concordance for *over* and *above*.

FIGURE 6 *Above* and *over* mean the same thing, don't they? Here is a concordance of the two words taken from the same corpus of texts. Study it, then answer the questions below.

```
 1  ow men but also with nature  and, above all, with those Higher Powers which
 2  ays, his dirty merino collar rose above his  shirt, and he smelled the same
 3  oad accidents have alcohol levels above the legal limit for  driving.  Drivi
 4  lights as well. If the red lights above your  lane flash, you must not go be
 5  es, for I saw her once as if from above, moving through a  kind of square, o
 6  state agency business. We now have over 160 offices under  the Cornerstone n
 7  ly injured are either  under 15 or over 60. The young and the elderly may no
 8  n unlikely  proposition. I did it, over a period of time, by having at least
09   . This process should be repeated over a two week period. If there are any
10  rveys divide teenagers  into those over and those under sixteen, which is th
11   late 1950s - went on being handed over every Friday until his death,  even
12  on of paying  for larger purchases over several months. The minimum amount p
13  child may do the same.   Don't be over-suspicious and try not to over react
14  s response. I got letters from all over the country,  from young mothers of
15  , as it were, throw  their rubbish over the fence into the neighbour's garde
16  ded  for pedestrians. Do not climb over the guard rails or walk outside them
17  use of the children we played with over the road was  given to the youngest
18  irls leave home.  When they've got over the shock, most are mainly con-  cer
19  eglect that I remember feeling was over the top at the  time) and tie a piec
20  eans work for dozens of people all over the world. And every year, hosts  an
21  to  many parts of Britain and met over thirty girls, mainly  in their home
22  that looks pretty good,' so I went over to the  ski jumps and just had a loo
23  s from local control and hand them over to unaccountable  bodies and private
24  do have problems, please talk them over with  Sister or the social worker. T
25   visitors all at once,  which will over-excite him. Some hospitals welcome b
27  s has worn off or the operation is over.   What you can do for your child i
28  tlessly - until it is suddenly all over.  The guests go home and the beautif
29  ed headlights on larger machines  (over 150cc - 200cc).   29  Do not drive
```

1. In which of the contexts of *above* (1 – 5) could you substitute *over*?

2. Make a list of the contexts in which *over* means:

   a. *at a higher level* or *covering* ....

   b. *more than* ....

   c. *from one side to the other* ....

   d. *during* (from beginning to end of a period of time) ....

   e. *finished* ....

3. What does *over-* mean when used as a prefix, as in numbers 13 and 25?

   ....

4. What do these phrasal verbs mean?

   hand over (11 and 23) ....

   get over (18) ....

   talk over (24) ....

5. What does *all over* mean in numbers 14 and 21?

   ....

6. What does *over the top* mean in number 19?

   ....

This exercise shows what can be done at a fairly high level (Intermediate or above) to exploit concordance output thoroughly in the detailed study of words. The keywords themselves are very common, but the concordance reveals information relating to aspects of vocabulary – nuances of meaning, style, idiom – which the more advanced learner needs to absorb, but which are rarely dealt with in such detail in standard coursebooks. But exercises of this sort need not be so complex. By paring down the same concordance output it is possible to create an exercise (or a part of a longer exercise) with much less ambitious objectives for Lower Elementary students. In Figure 7 the word processor has been used to delete all but a few selected contexts. (Most word processors will allow you to delete or copy an entire line of text at a time.)

FIGURE 7

```
1   state agency business. We now have over 160 offices under  the Cornerstone n
2   ly injured are either  under 15 or over 60. The young and the elderly may no
3   , as it were, throw  their rubbish over the fence into the neighbour's garde
4   ded  for pedestrians. Do not climb over the guard rails or walk outside them
5   to   many parts of Britain and met over thirty girls, mainly   in their home
```

1. In which of these examples does *over* mean *from one side to the other*?:

....

2. What does *over* mean in the other examples?

....

d Group work

When you run a concordance of a common item on a large corpus the output is inevitably very large. In order to make a manageable exercise you have to edit it drastically, thus losing valuable data. There is another solution, however, which is to divide the output into parts and distribute these among your learners as the basis of a group activity.

Figure 8 shows an exercise for Intermediate learners based on the concordance of *look*, *see* and *watch*, together with their various inflected forms, in ELTTEXT. Just a few contexts have been removed to reduce repetition (for example, there were more than ten instances of *see* used to refer to another part of a document, as in *see p. 101*). The remaining data are simply split into four sections of roughly equal size. This can be done with a pair of scissors; it does not require a word processor. These are incorporated into worksheets, each detailing the same tasks, which are distributed to four different groups of students. (The number of groups can be varied of course, according to the size of the output, the number of learners in the class and the amount of time available.)

The lesson is conducted in three stages.

Stage A: Divide the class into groups (see above) and hand out the worksheets.

Stage B: The groups work independently, completing the tasks on the worksheet. They are encouraged to use dictionaries. Although they work together, every individual must make a note of the answers in order to be able to participate in stage B.

Stage C: New groups are formed in which all of the original groups are represented. Thus if there are 12 students in the class, and therefore three in each of the original groups, there will be three groups of four in the new configuration. An easy way to manage this is to ask each of the original groups to allocate a number to each of its members: 1, 2 and 3, then to designate an area of the room for each number: " Number ones over here please, twos over there and threes over there". This ensures an even distribution. Any extra students can choose which group to join.

In the new groups students compare their findings from stage A. They compile a complete list of phrasal verbs (task B.1) and formulate an explanation of the way in which each verb differs in meaning from the other two (task B.2). They compare their explanations with the definitions and examples given for *look*, *see* and *watch* in their dictionaries. If they have more than one different dictionary they decide which one corresponds most closely with their own findings.

Stage D: Each group reports back briefly to the class.

FIGURE 8   Stage A:

1. (Pre-reading task) Before you look at your printout, try to answer this question in your group:

    What are the differences between *look*, *see* and *watch*? Make a note of these, with examples if you like.

2. Now look at your printout. Do the examples support what you said in 1? Put a cross by any examples that are not covered by your notes.

3. Make a note of any phrasal verbs formed with *look*, *see* or *watch* that you find.

Stage B:

Now get together with the other groups and compare notes.

1. Write a list of phrasal verbs formed with *look*, *see* and *watch*.

2. Write a short note about each verb to explain how it differs from the other two. Choose one or two good examples from the printouts to illustrate your explanations.

3. Compare your explanations with the definitions and examples in your dictionary. While you have your dictionary open, look up the meaning of any phrasal verbs that you are not sure about.

Group (a)

```
1 actical and emotional problems and watched as she struggled to bring up a ba
2 rs, especially girls, preferring to see them as innocent  children, so conse
3 hem and would not be without them. looking back, they would have done a few
4 ers so other people can read it and see what others have gone through. I lik
5 e were excluded because he couldn't see them stiff and proper quite fitting
6 ot dimmer and dimmer and finally he saw them only as through the one winking
7  many papers tied with string that looked official and held no interest. And
8  himself. He also did not appear to see too well and this the boy liked, for
9 s shook so much that the boy would watch in fascination as more often than n
10his presence. Then after a while he saw that the man noticed him in a sly ki
11ably the uncle's age though now he looked twice as old. He would spend endle
12is: it was the way the man used to watch him. Even in those days before he b
13 instinctively that for one man to look at another man like that was sinful.
14e yard - feeding the young calves, looking after the chickens, helping the a
15h his chores he could feel the man watching him, would turn suddenly and the
16 would be. He knew the man was not watching the chickens or what he was doin
17ckens or what he was doing. He was watching him. And watching him the way he
```

Group (b)

```
18as doing. He was watching him. And watching him the way he should be watchin
19 watching him the way he should be watching a woman. Bro. Justice went out o
20t herself to plead with her please look after the little boy. But the aunt,
21ing at all but was surreptitiously watching him beneath half-closed eyes. At
22e room again.   So he continued to watch the man and to visit the room while
23. But now he knew that the man was watching him, he grew more conscious of h
24 would go and stand by the bed and look down on the unshaven face and try to
25ding so close to him was no longer looking coy or foolish. His hair was stan
26ring the eye of the spirit level he saw the man advance towards him.  He ste
27t have shifted several times, for I saw her once as if from above, moving th
28d point of the dream where I stood watching her, left forefront.  She wore t
29and started to go round and round, looking out at me as she turned. I wish I
30emed right. I understood what I had seen in the dream when I learned the wor
31bably: the puzzlement of the child watching from the pavement, wondering wha
32ing on the platform with her family seeing her off, for the through train to
33t the Somme, she managed that to , looking after the three-year old my mothe
34 right for him; he doesn't have to look after you'), and I wish I could tell
35ack suede shoes, her lipstick. She looked so much better than the fat, sprea
36cked amazement of one who had never seen what she knew written down before.
37t her and her mother long before I looked them both in the face, or heard ab
38nd to have achieved viability if he saw that it was rapidly consuming its ca
39understand the problem and begin to see the possibility of evolving a new li
40rmanence. Produc- tivity will then look after itself. In industry, we can in
41following chapter is an attempt to look at the whole situa- tion again, from
42d be universal prosperity. One may look in vain for historical evidence that
```

Group (c)

```
43e. That is why I don't eat flesh. I see no need for killing.   There are incr
44these, choose a place where you can see clearly along the roads in all direc
45and always give drivers a chance to see you clearly.   2 Stand on the pavemen
46om traffic, but where you can still see if anything is coming. If there is n
47of the road but where you can still see traffic coming.   3  Look all round f
48om all directions, so take care to look along every road. And listen, too, b
49traffic near, let it go past. Then look round again and listen to make sure
50oss the road - don't run.  6  Keep looking and listening for traffic while y
51ng and listening in case you didn't see some traffic - or in case other traf
52ss.   Once you're in the road, keep looking and listening in case you didn't
53 When you cross at a road junction look out for traffic turning the corner,
54you.  Crossing at a Zebra crossing (see illustration page 60)  10 If there i
55nd pedal cyclists plenty of time to see you and to slow down and stop before
56 has stopped, walk across but keep looking both ways and listening in case a
57orcyclists or pedal cyclist has not seen you and tries to overtake a vehicle
58strian signals, obey them. If not, watch both the lights and the traffic and
59hen the lights are red remember to look out for turning traffic, and remembe
60ge of the vehicles where you can be seen by drivers, motorcyclists and pedal
61d pedal cyclists and where you can look all round for traffic. Then continue
62ear a street light where you can be seen more easily. Remember that it is mo
63it is more difficult for drivers to see you at night or in poor light, so wh
64ES  23  Keep out of the road if you see or hear ambulances, fire engines, po
65boots and gloves. To help others to see you, wear something light- coloured
66 off, always use your mirrors; but look round as well for a final check. Sig
67rrors (motorcyclists should always look behind, even if they have mirrors fi
```

To some extent the nature of the information gap that is engendered between groups will depend on the way in which the output has been sorted. In the above example a concordance has been taken of all parts of all three verbs simultaneously (*look**, *see*, *sees*, *seen*, *saw*, *watch**) and then printed out in order of occurrence. Because of this the data distributed to the respective groups differs somewhat because it originates from different texts (for example, groups (c) and (d) have all the instances from the Highway Code). Right sorting would bring together collocations, so that different uses or meanings of the verbs would tend to be distributed unevenly between the groups (one group might have all the instances of *look at*, for example). Sorting on the keyword would tend to distribute the verbs themselves among the groups. Left sorting to a depth of two or more should ensure a more or less random distribution.

Group (d)

```
68 two-wheelers are much less easy to see than larger vehicles and that their
69op well within the distance you can see to be clear. Go much more slowly if
70- it can be especially difficult to see pedestrians and cyclists at night an
71 crowded shopping streets, when you see a bus stopped, or near a parked milk
72 58  Drive slowly near schools and look out for children getting on or off b
73coming to a Zebra crossing, keep a look out for pedestrians waiting to cross
74ve special passing places. When you see a vehicle coming towards you, or the
75ine. do not cross it unless you can see the road well ahead is clear.   71  W
76are on a motorcycle or pedal cycle look behind and to your off-side. Signal
77s overtaking traffic queues should look out for pedestrians crossing between
78ween you and any oncoming vehicle; look out for cyclists, motorcyclists and
79the position of the other vehicle, watch carefully for traffic approaching o
80hills where they may not be able to see. If your herd is very large, divide
81r may be present even if you cannot see the cause.  Stopping and parking  18
82ever drive on to one unless you can see the road is clear o the other side.
83d lights. At such crossings, stop, look both ways, listen and make sure ther
84his country it's still very rare to see black television presenters, and bla
85ing the centre of the stage. I you look at the previous prime ministers we'v
86d me during the emergency' and she looked at him and said, 'and I may very w
87you know those are great moments to see people of that kind of power and and
88f other drums - the drum kit as you see in pop groups and umm umm and then r
89s reaction of my teacher was, well look at these marks they're not very good
90ps you might want to go through and see what he says; and so the percussion
91on teacher said well I can't really see why she she shouldn't be playing per
92r could take her out to dinner, you see; and so we went up to the mountain o
```

e Gapfill
exercises

So far all the exercises we have seen in this chapter have required the learner to supply information about the keyword, using clues present in the contexts. The reverse of this procedure is to ask the learner to supply the keyword itself. A concordance output can be turned into a gapfill exercise by simply deleting the keyword. This can be done without a word processor (a bottle of correcting fluid will suffice), but a more elegant presentation can be achieved by replacing the keyword, using the word processor's "search and replace" facility, with a row of spaces, dots or underscores.

The advantage of using concordance output for this purpose can be seen in Figure 9. Few of the contexts point unambiguously to the answer, but cumulatively they enable the astute learner to eliminate competing possibilities.

Concordance output as teaching material

FIGURE 9   Can you identify the missing keyword in each of the following printouts?

1. ....

```
* lay?  <Evelyn:> Well. Percussion _____ covers 600 and over 650 instrument
* 't _____ hit people and don't _____ kill people, er, permeates and the
* t would the change in legal form _____ mean?  A  Instead of a mutual inst
* ace to let him pass, the man had _____ reached out and lightly touched hi
* e of twelve I had a bit of a job _____ starting percussion because er whe
* luence that they, British people _____ think that other countries are les
* over 650 instruments and umm I I _____ try and play as many as I can but
```

2. ....

```
* capital easier.  Q  If you had to _____ in one short sentence "Why PLC?" w
* ible with him in hospital you can _____ step by step what is happening. Ma
*  less strange if you are there to _____ what is happening in words he unde
* ible and comprehensible; they can _____, or show to children what they do
* s fall in pregnancy rate has been _____ed by the greater use of contracept
* surroundings show, and nothing is _____ed. It is also about a period of re
```

3. ....

```
*  can either settle your account in _____ by writing one cheque, or just pay p
*  many greetings cards. Most are in _____ colour and some have distinctive gol
* tely to the nearest VISA bank. For _____ details and a written quotation plea
*  Servicing & Valet Leaflet, giving _____ details of all our services, will be
*  You can enjoy your holiday to the _____ knowing that if something does go wr
*  It is a rich and various cuisine, _____ of many marvellous dishes with defin
*  competing, be able to provide the _____ range of personal financial services
* ember setting out our proposals in _____.  Q  In 1986, the Members voted by a
```

4. ....

```
* t is in many ways - in London - an _____ and a tolerant society.  <Interviewe
* ng. If the green light is showing, _____ both gates or fully raise both barri
* in and Ireland.  Think of it as an _____ door  A door into the world of books
*  doors, the doors of his mind flew _____ one after another, like living insid
* g distance shown below. But on the _____ road, in good conditions, a gap of o
* our side lights on as well. Do not _____ the doors nearest to the carriageway
* r new purpose-built Service Centre _____, day and night, is the ideal answer
*  concentration, his mouth slightly _____. At other times he simply sat still
```

5. ....

```
* sham & Brighton. Follow A23 north _____ Gatwick until roundabout. Take fir
* ustice, remembering Job, softened _____ him, although he still care- fully
* irit level he saw the man advance _____ him.  He stepped backwards, his he
* she turned and came some way back _____ me, admonishing, shaking her finge
* low signs to Crawley. Return back _____ the airport, driving under Termina
*  miles an hour and we were coming _____ the bottom and on the ... at the b
* eques from TSB you could win £400 _____ the cost of your holiday. Ask at y
* han him; so I took off, was going _____ the finish but er going in the air
* es. When you see a vehicle coming _____ you, or the driver behind you want
```

An interesting twist can be introduced by basing the exercise on a mixed concordance; that is, one in which the contexts of two or more headwords are jumbled. This can be done by mixing together lines from different output files by using a word processor or, more rapidly, by specifying two or more keywords in the original search, if the concordancer will allow this.

In the exercise in Figure 10 the learner knows which words have been deleted and simply has to place them in the right context. However, there is a follow-up task designed to exploit the data more fully.

FIGURE 10

```
1   daily life. It is more often the  ____ conditions that many young mothers a
2   he had nothing else, he was still ____ because he had this space which allo
3   in the 1950s. We believed we were ____ because we children were expensive i
4   of 'education for leisure' in the ____ countries, and of 'the transfer of t
5   the transfer of technology' to the ____ countries.  The liquidation of these
6   , power- ful or powerless, ____ or ____, influential or uninfluential. To ta
7   e has nothing to gain. Are not the ____, the exploited, the oppressed most 1
8    our own flesh. The message to the ____ and discontented is that they must n
9   ough from time to time to help the ____, because this is the way by which th
10  at far off when everybody would be ____. We shall then, he said, 'once more
11  a substitute for anything. It is a ____ and various cuisine, full of many ma
12  is phenomenal! Nearly all nuts are ____ in pro- tein,as are many seeds.  In
13  The palate should find variety in ____ and light, sharp and mild But also c
14  from serving two or three courses ____ with cream and eggs, or a sweet tart
15  drivers to see you at night or in ____ light, so when visibility is ____, w
16  ____ light, so when visibility is ____, wear something light-coloured or br
17  sors) at night or in conditions of ____ visibility.  33  Tinted glass does n
18  ions, or where the road surface is ____. Do not overtake motorcycles, pedal
```

1. In the above concordance output the keywords *rich* and *poor* have been removed. Can you put them back in the right contexts?

2. Make a note of all the contexts where *rich* or *poor* are used metaphorically (that is, where they do not mean "having a lot of money" and "having very little money"). What do the two words mean in their metaphorical senses?

RICH: ....

POOR: ....

f Re-ordering the left or right context

Concordance output can also be turned into matching-up exercises. The example in Figure 11 is based on a partial concordance of *such* in which the right contexts have been shuffled. This was done with a word processor by deleting every right context in turn and copying it into a different location. If your word processor has sophisticated "cut and paste" facilities you can do this more rapidly as follows. Cut out all the right contexts as a block and copy this to another file. Sort this file alphabetically. This effectively shuffles the lines (unless the output was sorted alphabetically on the right context in the first place, in which case you should sort in reverse alphabetical order). Finally, paste the block back into its original location.

FIGURE 11 In this concordance something seems to have gone wrong with the printer! The contexts after the word *such* have come out in the wrong order. Can you put them back in order so that the first part of each context matches the second part? Write a number in the brackets at the end of each context to show which ending goes with each beginning. The first one has been done for you.

```
 1   Burnley; 'but think how she felt, such things  as salad, vegetables and bre (12)
 2  d not mind. To him the old man was such thing as a ones meal. The recipes th (..)
 3  nd this applies to other countries such  richness of choice that a Book Toke (..)
 4  r on clothes. - Empty containers, such  as his nickname or what foods he lik(..)
 5  the road to warn drivers at places such a little girl, she was only  eleven, (..)
 6  ything  she should know about him, such as aerosols or tins.  A combination  (..)
 7   gifts animals give us painlessly. such times the boy did not laugh. He was  (..)
 8  thin  a year or two from illnesses such dinners, optimism is restored, and o (..)
 9  e remains. Friend-  ships bloom at such as skin cancer or pneumonia which th (..)
10  ct under the sun. This is world of such as Aus-  tralia, New Zealand and Can (..)
11  dish-Suppers    There really is no such an  object of fascination that he se (..)
12  red accompaniment to the meat, are such  as bends and brows of hills where t (..)
13  d rosewood and mahogany  floor. At such as milk and eggs.   The proposition (..)
```

To complete the exercise successfully the learners have to detect lexical clues which link left and right contexts (*Empty containers . . . aerosols or tins*). However they will also inevitably have their attention drawn to the existence of two distinct structures: *such* + NP, referring back to something which has previously been named, and *such as* + NP, used to introduce one or more examples.

g Exercises based on learner texts

As we saw in Chapter 2, a concordancer can be a useful diagnostic tool for identifying common errors in learners' writing. Taking the process a step further, we can use those errors, or rather the contexts in which they occur, as the basis for remedial exercises.

The exercise in Figure 12 was designed to help advanced students to improve their academic writing. The examples were taken from a whole-sentence concordance of *which*, *who* and *that* run on a corpus of student essays.

FIGURE 12
The sentences below all contain relative pronouns. In some cases a participle connector could be used to better effect. Working with a partner, show how you would rewrite each sentence using a participle connector. If you think the sentence does not need rewriting simply put a tick under it.

1. Based on the information that we get from current studies of health implications of computing, we would like to make a conclusion whether there is a potential hazard of computers or not.

   "...information obtained from..."

2. But in the case of carbon certain compounds which have the same molecular structure exist in different forms because they have either different arrangements in space or their atoms are linked together in a different way.

3. Further studies in this field led to a new branch of science that we called "ergonomics" or "human factors".

4. There is no higher body which can rule over a sovereign state without its consent.

5. Indeed there are over two million known organic compounds which contain carbon and hydrogen but also oxygen, nitrogen, sulphur and many other elements.

6. Over the past decade computer users have reported a variety of health complaints that have been associated with computers including visual and musculoskeletal discomfort, pain, and psychological distress.

7. The third chapter provides a survey of racemil modification which is a mixture of equal parts of enantiomers, followed by a detailed discussion of the resolution of racemil modification.

8. These requirements achieve a critical importance in devices which utilize heterostructure with very thin layers (10-150A) and abrupt compositional interface like, for instance, the quantum well lasers.

9. This means that network planning is not formulated as a single objective problem, but as a problem that concerns the inclusion of multiple objectives into the process.

10. Today there are millions of people world-wide who use computers in their daily work.

Conclusion

A concordancing program combined with a suitable corpus of texts can be an excellent source of raw material for written language exercises. With the aid of a word processor, an enterprising teacher can manipulate that material so as to create a variety of exercise-types. In this chapter we have considered just a few examples of such exercise-types. The possibilities certainly do not end here. By experimenting with your own texts and with your own learners in mind, you are almost certain to gain new insights into the language you are teaching and to devise new approaches to teaching it.

Chapter summary

■ The output from a concordancer can easily be turned into language teaching material, either by editing with a word processor or by old-fashioned scissors and paste methods.

■ Whether or not you can produce materials for specific purposes will depend on the size and contents of your corpus. It is generally best to look at the concordance for a particular item with an open mind before deciding what use you can make of it.

■ We have seen examples of exercises of the following types:

　– deducing the meaning of the keyword from context

　– study of grammatical features of particular words (and of general grammatical features) via the concordance of groups of associated words

　– study of homonyms and synonyms

　– group work activities in which concordance output is distributed among various groups who subsequently pool their impressions and conclusions

　– gapfill exercises

　– matching exercises, in which the left or right contexts are jumbled and have to be re-instated

　– remedial exercises based on learners' own writing

5 *Interactive uses of Concordancing*

This chapter deals with interactive uses of concordancing software and personal computers. Part 1 briefly describes a basic set of requirements for PC-based classroom research, including the main types of concordancing software currently available, and the types of text resources appropriate for such work. Parts 2, 3 and 4 give examples of lessons with various levels of learner that draw on a computer in the classroom as a principal resource.

Classroom research

Previous chapters in this book have considered concordancing software as a tool for teachers. All of the examples have been of paper-based activities and the computer has very much been in the hands of the teacher, not of the learner. We still need, therefore, to discuss one of the most exciting possibilities that concordancing makes available. For it is now possible to give students the opportunity to engage in a real form of computer-based classroom research. If you are able to give your students access to a PC you can also give them the chance to discover rules of language use for themselves.

1 What do you need?

Once you have gained access to a computer, the next step is to work out how to build the technology into both syllabus and methodology.

The computer or computers available to your students may be in a study centre/library, dedicated computer room or your own classroom. The machines may be stand-alone, with or without hard-disks, or networked. The characteristics of your particular machine and its location will present certain limitations (Do you need to timetable access or can you be spontaneous? How quickly can the computer run?) but a more important constraint will be the type of concordancing program you are working with.

a Software

We have already mentioned (Chapter 1) that the three main types of concordancing software currently available can be divided into three types. **Streaming concordancers** "read" a text line-by-line and produce concordanced text either to screen, printer or disk as they chunk through the documents you are analyzing. **Text indexers** create an index of your text in one (sometimes lengthy) operation and then permit a large variety of text retrieval activities, including concordancing. **In-memory concordancers** read the whole text into memory and then proceed to operate on it.

For interactive classroom research these different types of software all have their advantages and disadvantages. The most important things to bear in mind when you are planning to get your students to work with concordancers are: How much time is it going to take to get the information in which you are interested? How much time is it going to take for students to learn how to use the software?

b Data

Next you will need data. Here it becomes a question of what you have to hand, and what your objectives are. For example, if you are working with an Upper Intermediate class and want to help them improve their written English, concordancing can be very helpful in teaching how to remove redundant pronouns, auxiliaries and so forth after a conjunction. In this case a mixed bag of documents produced within your organization (administrative material from which names and confidential information have been removed or text that teachers have typed on the school word processor) could be ideal. If, by contrast, you want a group of University level learners to study appropriate linking devices (sentence conjuncts, relative pronouns, participles) then a body of formal discursive writing will be needed.

c Display

Finally, you will also need to decide on how you will display your information. It is of little use to set students a task that requires them to note specific points when the concordance output scrolls up the screen at an impossible speed, never to be seen again. If you can predict that a search is going to produce a considerable amount of data, it is much better to direct it to a disk file that the students can then work on in a word processor.

The other main option is to direct the output immediately to a printer. If you do this it is worth remembering that you can print out more context for the keyword if you select a smaller character for the printer. With most modern equipment this can be done through a control panel on the front of the machine. If you choose a condensed typeface (17 or 20 cpi) you can get contexts of up to 160 characters onto a line with standard A4 paper. If you choose the usual default font size of 10 cpi this context is reduced to 79. If the printer is set in a draft mode it should be able to keep up with the concordancer fairly well and will provide information that students can begin to discuss immediately.

2 Examples of applications A:

Learning about grammar

context:

- **learners:**   General English: Lower Intermediate students
- **class size:**   24 – 30
- **time available:**   2 x 40 minutes (over two weeks)
- **facilities:**   – 1 PC + an "in memory" concordancer
  - mixed collection of word-processed formal writing (e.g. essays, reports)

learning objective: to increase learners' understanding of the position of adverbs in English

lesson plan:

Stage 1: Students select words for study from a reading passage

Different groups in the class are given reading passages which contain examples of adverbs being studied by students as part of their English Language syllabus. As an initial activity, learners are asked to underline as many adverbs as they can find. This provides a simple check of their recognition knowledge and makes it possible to teach/revise words that are unfamiliar to them. An example is given in Figure 1:

FIGURE 1

I remember when I was about 19. I went to a dance at the village hall. I went with my best friend, Marjorie. Marjorie was very pretty and all the boys liked her. They all wanted to dance with her. I didn't enjoy dances very much. I was always very shy.

I sat at a table in the corner of the dance floor. No one asked me to dance. After about an hour, Marjorie came up to me and said, "Go and ask one of the boys to dance. You can't just sit there!" It was awful. I hated every minute of it. In the end she told one of her boyfriends to go and ask me for a dance. I was so embarrassed! Anyway, the boy came up and we danced. His name was Mick and he was very nice ... "

(from *Opening Strategies* Abbs and Freebairn, 1982, Longman)

This text could give a set of adverbs such as the following: *just, very, always, when, about.*

Stage 2: Concordances produced by groups for each set of targets

Once a list of words has been selected by the different groups of students, they can be set the task of producing concordances for their wordlist and then analyzing their information. With a reasonably varied set of corpus material it is possible to produce illuminating examples through student research. The learners have to decide how to display their information, whether to sort to the left or the right, and how much context they need to show. Each group can be given a report form like the one in Figure 2 to complete, as a means of helping them organize their data.

FIGURE 2

KEYWORD: _____ adverb

LEFT SORT ....

Are there any words (or word classes) that appear frequently before the keyword? Write any that you find below:

RIGHT SORT ....

Are there any words (or word classes) that appear frequently after the keyword? Write any that you find below:

Are there any grammar rule/s that you think might work for this word? Write them in the box below and then decide how you can test your idea by studying further examples.

Stage 3: Students report on results (e.g. position/collocation of target)

Concordance printouts for *always* that students have created are given in Figures 3, 4 and 5 (data drawn from ELTTXT6 and ELTTXT7).

FIGURE 3

```
oastguard stations.    Make sure you always park your vehicle safely and where it
witch off the engine and headlamps. Always lock your vehicle.    130 Never park o
k on the road in fog. Lights should always be left on in these conditions.    131
ing.    139 Before starting to ride, always look round and make sure that it is s
 to pass or pulling up at the kerb, always look behind and make sure it is safe.
larger vehicles and that you should always give clear arm signals to let drivers
ons.    145 When you are riding: a) always keep both hands on the handlebar unle
dlebar unless you are signalling; b) always keep both feet on the pedals; c do no
  These signals are for your safety. Always act on them. Remember - danger may be
d twin flashing red traffic lights. Always obey these traffic lights and stop at
s no train coming before you cross. Always "Give Way" to trains.    HORSE RIDERS
.   So when you leave your vehicle, always:   - Remove the ignition key and enga
d in politics? <Diane Abbott:> I've always been interested in politics, as um, f
ntence 'cause the Today programme I always say is the place to drop a word in th
er ... interviewing politicians is always entertaining because they always have
is always entertaining because they always have something to say and they come i
 sleep in the afternoon but I don't always manage that. But I don't find that di
g people and umm er my parents have always you know lived on farms and my ol
```

FIGURE 4

```
g people and umm er my parents have always you know lived on farms and my oldest
s no train coming before you cross. Always "Give Way" to trains.    HORSE RIDERS
  These signals are for your safety. Always act on them. Remember - danger may be
k on the road in fog. Lights should always be left on in these conditions.    131
d in politics? <Diane Abbott:> I've always been interested in politics, as um, f
er ... interviewing politicians is always entertaining because they always have
larger vehicles and that you should always give clear arm signals to let drivers
is always entertaining because they always have something to say and they come i
dlebar unless you are signalling; b) always keep both feet on the pedals; c do no
ons.    145 When you are riding: a) always keep both hands on the handlebar unle
witch off the engine and headlamps. Always lock your vehicle.    130 Never park o
ing.    139 Before starting to ride, always look round and make sure that it is s
 to pass or pulling up at the kerb, always look behind and make sure it is safe.
 sleep in the afternoon but I don't always manage that. But I don't find that di
d twin flashing red traffic lights. Always obey these traffic lights and stop at
oastguard stations.    Make sure you always park your vehicle safely and where it
ntence 'cause the Today programme I always say is the place to drop a word in th
   So when you leave your vehicle, always:   - Remove the ignition key and enga
```

FIGURE 5

```
ons.    145 When you are riding:  a) always keep both hands on the handlebar unle
dlebar unless you are signalling; b) always keep both feet on the pedals; c do no
s no train coming before you cross. Always "Give Way" to trains.    HORSE RIDERS
   sleep in the afternoon but I don't always manage that. But I don't find that di
g people and umm er my parents have always you know lived on farms and my oldest
witch off the engine and headlamps. Always lock your vehicle.    130 Never park o
ntence 'cause the Today programme I always say is the place to drop a word in th
d in politics? <Diane Abbott:> I've always been interested in politics, as um, f
er ... interviewing politicians is always entertaining because they always have
   to pass or pulling up at the kerb, always look behind and make sure it is safe.
d twin flashing red traffic lights. Always obey these traffic lights and stop at
ing.    139 Before starting to ride, always look round and make sure that it is s
   These signals are for your safety. Always act on them. Remember - danger may be
larger vehicles and that you should always give clear arm signals to let drivers
k on the road in fog. Lights should always be left on in these conditions.    131
is always entertaining because they always have something to say and they come i
.    So when you leave your vehicle, always:    - Remove the ignition key and enga
oastguard stations.    Make sure you always park your vehicle safely and where it
```

The group working on *always* then came up with the report sheet in Figure 6 overleaf.

It takes students a little time to become used to working this way, but once they are familiar with the software you have available and the different ways you can report your results, grammar lessons take on a new dimension.

Stage 4: Students prepare gap-fill exercises to test other groups

Once learners have had a chance to report back on their findings they can prepare simple gap-fill tests for their fellow students. These can be prepared on a word processor by mixing the files they have been working with and then removing keywords, or by cutting and pasting and then photocopying.

FIGURE 6

KEYWORD:		adverb

LEFT SORT ....

Are there any words (or word classes) that appear frequently before the keyword? Write any that you find below:

RIGHT SORT ....

Are there any words (or word classes) that appear frequently after the keyword? Write any that you find below:

Are there any grammar rule/s that you think might work for this word? Write them in the box below and then decide how you can test your idea by studying further examples.

3 Examples of applications B:

a Vocabulary development: adverbs and adjective collocations

A concordancer can provide a very useful way of raising learners' awareness of the ways in which words go together.

context:

■ learners: General English Intermediate/Upper Intermediate students

■ time available: 2 x 1.5 hours

■ facilities: – ideally, a computer room with enough PCs for one machine per three or four students + "in-memory" concordancing program

              – small corpus of mixed native speaker writing

learning objective: to look at some of the ways in which adjectives are qualified and extend the learners' knowledge of collocational restrictions on common adverbs

lesson plan:

Stage 1: Learners find out what adjectives exist in their document by creating a wordlist

Working in groups, learners create wordlists for the texts they have available. These will be similar to Figure 7. Learners will find out quite quickly that there are relatively few adjectives in the very high frequency sections of their wordlists. In a small corpus of about 40,000 words, they will probably have to look in the frequencies of below 7 or 8 before they find significant numbers of adjectives.

FIGURE 7

afterwards	6	changes	6
air	6	close	6
already	6	cold	6
angry	6	competition	6
anyone	6	contraception	6
babies	6	cooking	6
beginning	6	council	6
birthday	6	credit	6
Burnley	6	cry	6
call	6	details	6
cash	6	discovered	6

The next step is for learners to identify and select the adjectives they want to study. With an in-memory concordancer it is possible to make the selection on screen and to obtain the concordance lines for the selected words directly. (With the other types of concordancers it may be necessary to make the selection on paper and then to key in the new wordlist for concordancing – a rather more laborious process if the list is long.)

Figure 8 shows the selection of adjectives chosen by one group of learners working in this way.

FIGURE 8

alone	different	good	less	pregnant	vegetarian
angry	difficult	great	little	public	welcome
available	early	happy	local	rich	whole
best	easy	hard	long	round	wide
big	economic	high	natural	secret	wrong
black	expensive	hot	new	sexual	young
clean	fair	human	old	simple	
close	familiar	important	open	special	
common	fine	increasing	personal	sudden	
competitive	free	large	poor	terrible	
dangerous	full	last	possible	upset	

The concordance on this list was very large. It also contained a large number of unmodified adjectives. Figure 9 gives a small extract which demonstrates this problem.

FIGURE 9

```
with me, and so forth, no way was I to be alone in London, was the message, for instance.
e from them as the furthest star. The boy alone had been able to enter his world, question
iving on social security benefits, living alone, getting married, and much more. Each chap
icularly if you are doing the preparation alone  Finally, try to do most what you do best
d held no interest. And as long as he was alone in this room he was happy because he knew
 world. The boy simply was.   He was also angry at the boy's defection because, simply, he
  I mean there wa-... it wasn't really an angry exchange at all. Umm and when I listened t
 ed. Sometimes parents are very upset and angry, but only very occasionally do they take t
```

Stage 2: Learners identify and record those adjectives that are qualified by an adverb

Learners next designed a secondary search (using the "proximity" search facility in the concordancer) that let them look for all occurrences of adjectives that were linked with an adverb. They were encouraged to use their knowledge of morphology in English to devise a search pattern that looked for occurrences of *ly to the left of the keyword. They then extended this to include words such as *quite, pretty, very*. This was not seen as definitive, but it did give useful results. An extract from the concordance file they produced is shown in Figure 10. The list of adverbs they derived from this concordance is given in Figure 11.

FIGURE 10

```
it effortlessly and thoughtlessly like the old man. The man also had lucid times, when he
-six I think but he was really ... :> Very old. :> Very old, yeah, I mean ancient! But he
but he was really ... :> Very old. :> Very old, yeah, I mean ancient! But he was the super
ub there er -lent me a pair of old, really old boots, and er they said, 'Look there's a te
trial processes, have produced an entirely new situation - a situation resulting not from
cking on a bit now. I've recently signed a new contract which will take me up to the age o
ars.   A Yes, but we have clearly seen the new competitive attacks on our markets. A few y
 beans and whole grains are also extremely good protein sources. Buckwheat is phenomenal!
nds. The point is, very few people dislike good food it seems, and if you give them just t
uinea pigs, and I can safely report that a good time was had by all, though few of our fri
 well look at these marks they're not very good, and umm but I said well really I I play t
d after about a month I was getting pretty good, 'cos I was a good skier anyway but after
hought. 'Well, you know, that looks pretty good,' so I went over to the ski jumps and just
urf start watering. Give the area a really good soaking (water should pass into the underl
```

FIGURE 11

easily	increasingly	really
entirely	most	relatively
equally	ordinarily	significantly
extremely	particularly	slightly
highly	pretty	very
impatiently	quite	

Stage 3: Learning about use and restrictions

In the last stage of this work the learners went on to find out about the ways in which these adverbs were used and to see how they changed the meanings of the keywords. Working with two grids they recorded i) which keywords were used with each adverb and ii) whether the adverb made the keyword stronger or weaker. This work was shared out between groups of four (there were 16 in the class) and groups reported back to each other at the end of the session. The report back form of Group A was similar to Figure 12.

FIGURE 12

	occurs with	strengthener	weakener	other
easily	available	✓	–	–
entirely	new	✓	–	–
equally	important	–	–	✓
extremely	good	✓	–	–
	difficult	✓	–	–
	dangerous	✓	–	–
highly	competitive	✓	–	–
	competitive	✓	–	–
impatiently	upset	–	–	✓

Stage 4: Extension activities

As the students in the group shared information they began to recognize certain collocational patterns. They quickly spotted, for example, that some adverbs such as *very* and *extremely* appear to be used more freely than others such as *highly* and *impatiently*. This led them to ask questions about the range and restrictions of the others. What other words could be modified by *highly*? Or, for that matter, what other adverbs could be used to modify *competitive*.

Not surprisingly, this task usually provokes more questions than can be answered by the data in hand. The value of the activity is that it gets students asking the right kind of questions and shows how useful answers can be found through observation.

4 Examples of applications C:

The approach outlined in this section could be used in any ESP setting – the way of working remains the same whatever features you are looking for.

context:

- learners: undergraduate/post-graduate non EL specialist
- time available   2 x 1.5 hours
- facilities: – 1 or 2 PCs + "in-memory" concordancers
  - small corpus of machine-readable academic writing such as essays and dissertations (including reformulations) written by students of different nationalities as well as by English native-speakers.

learning objective: to establish an appreciation of appropriate use of sentence conjuncts in formal academic writing

lesson plan:

Stage 1: Comparing examples

The first stage in such an activity could be to compare samples of learner writing with native-speaker text as in Figure 13. Learners are initially asked if they can distinguish the non-native-speaker text from the native-speaker. Once they have worked this out they are asked to say if they can find any language items that are common to both sets of text but which are used differently.

FIGURE 13

- The subordinate, V. H. Bosanquet, was well aware of the region's ethnic composition – indeed, he appended to his report a revolutionary proclamation translated from Ukrainian – but he held, probably with reason, that "The (Ukrainian) peasant cares for no political question other than the improvement of his own condition, and the (local revolutionary) movement is therefore only political in so far as it has been exploited for political purposes".

- Because all files are simply a sequence of bytes, no structure is imposed on the file by the system. Therefore a user can easily construct files without concerning the file type.

- He had in mind a day when the Ukrainian part of Galicia could be detached from Austria-Hungary, taken out of Polish hands, and incorporated into the Russian Empire. The Ukrainian view of the matter, however, was not to go unheard.

- Most of the methods are used for obtaining the required monophase force vectors for exciting the required mode, and they are all based on the classical phase resonance condition which will be stated later. However, it has been shown that some of the methods had been successfully in separating and exciting the required mode for structures having acceptable level of modal densities, but nevertheless none of the methods have given much attention yet to the problems associated with the presence of non-linearity.

Here it is clear that there is a contrast between the ways in which one set of writers has used conjuncts when compared with the other. Students are able to distinguish between the text sources fairly easily, using collocation, grammar and appropriacy as clues. Finding the common element is sometimes more problematic but, with this level of learner, they are usually able to spot the way in which *however* and *therefore* occupy different positions in the different texts. The next stage is for students to derive wordlists from the corpora to hand (working with the native-speaker text in the first instance) and to see if there are other words that have a similar function to the two "linking" words they have been studying.

Stage 2: Wordlists

Figure 14 shows an extract from the sort of wordlist that students can produce with appropriate software. With its help it is possible for them to collect a second list of "linking words" that they will use in their research. They may be asked to draw up a checklist of connectors before studying the table or to consult standard grammar references and then see which connectors have been used in the texts. One such list is given in Figure 15.

FIGURE 14

personal	18	sometimes	15	few	13
problem	18	While	15	her	13
think	18	you'll	15	However	13
year	18	able	14	income	13
car	17	back	14	long	13
never	17	days	14	Mother	13
those	17	don't	14	offer	13
aunt	16	financial	14	often	13
before	16	give	14	problems	13

FIGURE 15

although	further	therefore
also	however	though
because	moreover	thus
besides	result	whether
consequence	similar	while
consequently	spite	whilst
due	thereby	yet

Stage 3: Analysis of "expert" writing and "learner" writing

Once the group has established the words it is going to study, it can be useful if two teams are designated to work respectively with native-speaker and non-native-speaker text corpora. They should collect information on the contexts in which their keywords arise, the positions they occupy in sentences or clauses and frequencies of occurrence for the corpora in question.

Stage 4: Reporting findings

The sorts of results which students come up with will, of course, depend on the data to hand. One study (Tribble, 1988) shows concordance data in which contrasts between expert writing (in this case data produced for academic

FIGURE 16

```
SPA.IN.  say perhaps when he was a boy.  However  another day he said that he
SPA.IN.  once I told you where it was.  However if you get lost you can alwa
SPA.IN.  re any question? - answer, No.  However if you have any questions, o
SPA.IN.  e life,  just the two of them.  However, things were not turning the
SPA.IN.  his belief in men  superiority.  However, in most of his tales such a
   .   .  ctor and his wife doesn't work.  However, she has  a lot of activitie
   .   .  n but in the different office.  However at the weekend often, we met
   .   .  We had a great time  together,  however we missed you!  The next tim
IIT.IN.  sn't always the best solution.  However, all depends on the method o
JAP.IN.  of frowers in  our big garden.  However, now her new long life begin
SSP.IN.  f  this kind used to be novels. However not alway does the films  sh
GSW.NT.  ble to read books.  Newspapers, however are not better. Although the
JAP.IN.  other words, it depends on you.  However, we can also say this  way.
PBR.IN.  e advertisements.  Newspapers, however consists of a number of larg
JAP.AD.  reached the college at 10.45.  However my tutor had not arrived yet


                    HOWEVER [native-speaker]


   the places in dispute. The treaty, however, only led to further difficulties
rance and England before his death. However, there are some important conside
llion, and coin, the king of Spain, however, reserving to himself a fourth pa
anish claims for an Italian empire, however much they might be opposed to the
le to hold it at all costs. Philip, however, not perhaps without some reason,
s generally held.' A little before, however, it had been objected by a member
ove advice'. A dssent was recorded, however, because' we look upon it as an E
pport the great burden of the war.. However, since it was presently evident t
   Their attempt to manage and drect, however, was repelled by Charles II, as i
orce Elizabeth paid,; she insisted, however, on regarding the States as respo
tain them. A letter from Buckhurst, however, made this clear, and Elizabeth i
rfeit of this Elysium. Their kauds, however, continued, and in October Leices
   the town. The rest of the  troops, however, were in- hard straits when money
' The main portion of the treasure  however, was paid out by poll. I have alr
```

journals) and the writing of EFL students is clearly demonstrated (see Figure 16). The contrast in this study was extreme. Work on less formal genres (e.g. journalism) would probably not show such a marked difference. This, however, does not reduce the interest of the insights that such close analysis can produce.

The same study went on to find similar patterning for the range of sentence conjuncts shown in Figure 17.

FIGURE 17

thereby	therefore
however	thus
moreover	while
nevertheless	yet

Discussion of these differences will focus on the fact that in the learner writing these conjuncts very often occur in front position. Learners can be asked to consider the range of possible positions for the set of conjuncts in their concordanced context, and to think about how they affect the weighting of the information in the text. Once learners see how the position of the conjunct directly affects the reader's experience of the writing they are in a much better position to write effectively and persuasively themselves.

Stage 5: Improving texts

Once students have become aware of the contrasts that often exist between "apprentice" and "expert" text through such research, text editing provides an excellent way of helping them develop greater control over the devices they have been studying. Mixed concordance printout can be a useful way to lead in to this – in Figure 18 there is an example of a concordance in which *because, however, although* and *therefore* have been combined.

FIGURE 18

```
t 1919.2 By the middle of the year, _____, Polish arms were prevailing over
gain, a prime concern of diplomats. _____ Galicia was far removed, geograp
ep abreast of developments, if only _____ Germany's ability to strike hard
 the balance.   Simpson was unable, _____, to change the views of his maste
, Before a revolt could take place, _____ both the Central Powers collapse
nlist British sympathy in 1912 only _____ he realized the fact.4 He decrie
 scope of his activity.4   The war, _____, dramatically altered both his own
he Poles and the Ruthenians'. Then, _____ he clouded the issue by claiming
y Raf- falovich spoke so vehemently _____ he had suffered on account of hi
local revolutionary] move- ment is, _____, only political in so far as it h
 particularly seriously in London.2 _____ Stepankivs'kyi, a prime mover amo
o the principle of nationality, and _____ throughout the peace-
 in the fluid politics of the east. _____ at first, only Austrian Ukraine
cide their own sovereignty'.? Soon, _____, the British Government had to thi
 called'The Ukraine Committee', and _____ this has been said to be a one-ma
a Ukrainian choir to visit Britain, _____ it would "a vertise the fact that
```

Further exercises can involve selective cloze on expert texts and reformulations of apprentice writing. They can finally be given a "sub-editing" task on a piece of learner writing such as Figure 19.

FIGURE 19   Work with a partner to improve this piece of student writing. Pay particular attention to the use of sentence conjuncts and the style and grammar of the piece.

Nuclear power is becoming more and more important energy resource in the modern world. Therefore, in the nuclear power station, the determining the distribution of neutrons is key and important. There are many methods to do it. Recently nodal methods developed by Jorn, et al. have more attractive features. They are computationally efficient than finite difference and finite element methods in the sense that they require shorter CPU times to comparable accuracy in the solutions. However, the nodal formalisms and the discrete-variable equations their produce are, in general, more complicated than their conventional counterparts. This, together with anticipated difficulties in applying the transverse-averaging procedure in curvilinear coordinates has limited the applications of nodal methods, so far, to Cartesian geometry.

In this paper we report recent progress in deriving and numerically implementing a nodal integral method for solving the neutron diffusion equation in cylindrical R-Z geometry. Also we represent comparisons of our numerical solutions to two short test problems with these obtained by the EX-2 code, which indicate the superior accuracy of the nodal integral method solutions on much coarser meshes.

5 Conclusion – letting go

This chapter has shown practical ways of using concordancers in the classroom. While the examples have been of highly-organized activities, some of the most exciting learning can take place as students become more confident in handling texts and machines and set off on their own.

Before moving on to free work, it can be very useful for students to undertake small tasks, where they are given specific problems to deal with, such as the following:

■ What metaphors in these texts employ colour – what effect do they have?

■ What idioms in these texts use parts of the body?

■ How often do native speakers break the rules about the use of commas around defining relative clauses – what is the effect of such rule-breaking?

Students will work together to devise ways of finding answers to these questions and use the concordancer as a way of collecting information. Once they are proficient in this sort of study, learners can go on to set up tasks that relate directly to their own interests and needs.

Students can investigate such areas as grammar, vocabulary, literature and style. If you have collected a corpus of learners' writing alongside a corpus of native-speaker writing your resources will be even more useful to your students. The investigative approaches used in this chapter work very well with open learning styles, and your students are sure to find ways of following up their own investigations.

Chapter summary

- The three main types of concordancing software presently available – **streaming concordancers**, **text indexers**, and **in-memory concordancers**, have contrasting uses in classroom research.

- Small collections of text (less than 50,000 words) are often best for classroom research as they do not take too long to process.

- These short texts generally provide get more information about grammar, syntax and function words than about individual lexical items.

- Concordancing programs can be used in the classroom with a wide variety of learners.

- Learners can either work directly from screen, recording their results on paper, or they can work from printouts produced during class time.

- Once learners have become confident at using concordancers they can develop their own research projects.

6 *Concordances and literature in foreign language teaching*

This chapter deals with some of the ways in which concordancing software can be used in the teaching of literature in EFL settings. Part 1 gives a brief introduction to the topic. Part 2 describes how concordances are used to help intermediate students to carry out a character analysis in a straightforward short story. Part 3 shows how concordancing can be of considerable help where more students are working with unusual writing.

1 Concordancing and literature

Much of the work done in recent years in author studies, stylistics and other branches of literary scholarship has benefited from the "number crunching" abilities of the computer, and it is beginning to be common for students of language and literature to have access to this sort of facility. There are public domain corpora of literary writing that include the Bible and Shakespeare and growing collections of machine-readable literary text from a variety of sources (see Appendix).

There are, however, many ways of using concordancing software which do not require the amassing of large quantities of text, and which can be very effective when working on literary writing with non-specialist students during an English Language course. The application of concordancing to the teaching of literature is a particularly fruitful area for classroom research and teaching/ learning. In particular, the short story and the lyric poem are wonderfully productive sources of material.

This chapter will show how concordancing can give learners insights into the structure of literary writing. It will also explain how concordancing can help in the traditional sorts of literary analysis (such as character analysis) that are common in public examinations, and how it gives learners a way of exploring literary uses of language. Even students without any previous background in literature can begin to understand the way a writer works with language and the effects that can be achieved across a text.

2 Teaching a short story: "The Fly" by Katherine Mansfield

The short story "The Fly" (1923), by the writer Katherine Mansfield (available in *The Collected Stories*, published by Penguin) is an ideal type of text for an Upper Intermediate class. It is only 2,100 words long and contains very little unusual vocabulary. At the simplest level of plot it recounts a meeting between two old men, in the course of which the main character (who is identified only as "the boss") is reminded of the death of his only son. This distresses him greatly, but as he tries to overcome his grief he notices a fly, trapped in the inkwell on his desk. First of all he rescues the insect. He then begins to study the fly closely and eventually starts to carry out an experiment which involves dropping blots of ink onto his late protégé. The fly dies and the old man finds he can no longer remember the source of his distress.

The story has three main sections. The opening is built round the conversation between "the boss" and his former employee, Woodifield, who has recently retired through ill-health. The second section deals with the boss's response to the grief he experiences when reminded of his son. The third describes the death of the fly. In an EFL class where some work on literature was taking place it would certainly be possible to ask learners to identify these sections and to provide an account of the main characters in the story. Concordance printouts would be very useful in both of these activities. Not only would they give the learners a very effective way into the story, they would also provide textual evidence with which to support their ideas.

b A lesson

Stage 1

Some pre-reading tasks could be set to help the learners deal with the story. These could include:

- Make a list of all the characters in the story. (if they do not include the boss's son, Woodifield's wife and daughter and the fly, ask them why!)

- Put the following events in sequence (1 – 5):

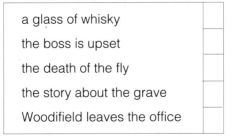

a glass of whisky	
the boss is upset	
the death of the fly	
the story about the grave	
Woodifield leaves the office	

Stage 2

If the learners have read the story before coming to the class, you could start by discussing some of their reactions to the story. You could ask them to:

■ say which sections they think they can recognize in the story. (They should justify their decisions.)

■ give their responses to the characters of "the boss" and Woodifield – what sort of people do they think they are? (They should be asked why they think the boss and his son are never named.)

Stage 3

At this point learners could be divided into groups of three or four and given concordance printouts on the words *boss* and *Woodifield*.

```
                                boss      26

MANS    13   a cigar and staring greedily at the boss, who rolled in his office chair, stout
MANS    18   t's comfortable enough," agreed the boss, and he flipped the Financial Times wi
MANS    40    he's on his last pins, thought the boss. And, feeling kindly, he winked at the
MANS    50   t have looked more surprised if the boss had produced a rabbit. "It's whisky, a
MANS    52   ky, ain't it?" he piped feebly. The boss turned the bottle and lovingly showed
MANS    54   u know," said he, peering up at the boss wonderingly, "they won't let me touch
MANS    58   it more that the ladies," cried the boss, swooping across for two tumblers that
MANS    73   ms." Old Woodifield paused, but the boss made no reply. Only a quiver in his ey
MANS    78   " "No, no!" For various reasons the boss had not been across. "There's miles of
MANS    92   uite right, quite right!" cried the boss, though what was right he hadn't the l
MANS    96   odifield was gone. For a moment the boss stayed, staring at nothing, while the
MANS    99    for half an hour, Macey," said the boss. "Understand? Nobody at all." "Very go
MANS   104   ing chair, and leaning forward, the boss covered his face with his hands. He wa
MANS   110   over six years had passed away, the boss never thought of the boy except as lyi
MANS   112   eep for ever. "My son!" groaned the boss. But no tears came yet. In the past, i
MANS   120    only son. Ever since his birth the boss had worked at building up this busines
MANS   142    might have happened yesterday. The boss took his hands from his face; he was p
MANS   148   ooked like that. At that moment the boss noticed that a fly had fallen into his
MANS   152   l back again and began to swim. The boss took up s pen, picked the fly out of t
MANS   165   y for life again. But just then the boss had an idea. He plunged his pen back i
MANS   173    a plucky little devil, thought the boss, and he felt a real admiration for the
MANS   177   inished its laborious task, and the boss had just time to refill his pen, to sh
MANS   180   e front legs were again waving; the boss felt a rush of relief. He leaned over
MANS   184   weak about its efforts now, and the boss decided that this time should be the l
MANS   190   not to be seen. "Come on," said the boss. "Look sharp!" And he stirred it with
MANS   193   ly to happen. The fly was dead. The boss lifted the corpse on the end of the pa
```

```
                              Woodifield      9

MANS    1  re very snug in here", piped old Mr Woodifield, and he peered out of the great,
MANS   12  o its last leaves. So there sat old Woodifield, smoking a cigar and staring gre
MANS   21   have it admired, especially by old Woodifield. It gave him a feeling of deep,
MANS   36  ing I wanted to tell you," said old Woodifield, and his eyes grew dim rememberi
MANS   63  oustaches, and cocked an eye at old Woodifield, who was silently rolling his in
MANS   73  ite near each other, it seems." Old Woodifield paused, but the boss made no rep
MANS   79  "There's miles of it", quavered old Woodifield, "and it's all as neat as a gard
MANS   95  he door and saw the old fellow out. Woodifield was gone. For a moment the boss
MANS  106  en a terrible shock to him when old Woodifield sprang that remark upon him abou
```

Initially working with *boss* they can be asked to identify the boundaries between the three main stages in the story. There may well be varying opinions, but this is all to the good. After discussion they should be able to agree on the area between lines 73 to 104 as representing one boundary (either the moment when Woodifield reminds the boss of his late son or the moment when the boss is alone in his office). The other boundary is represented by line 148 – "At that moment the boss noticed that a fly had fallen ... ".

Working with *boss* and *Woodifield* they can find out which verbs are used in connection with which character (i.e. with the character as the grammatical subject). If they write separate lists for each they will find:

boss

1.	2.	3.
rolled	covered	noticed
agreed	thought	took
thought	groaned	had
turned	had worked	felt
cried	took	thought
made		had
had not been		felt
cried		decided
stayed		said
said		lifted

Woodifield
piped
peered
staring
silently rolling
paused
quavered
gone

Here they can check their understanding of the characters by looking at the actions they are involved in. The contrast between the boss and Woodifield is heavily emphasized by the choice of verbs. *Cried* (in the jovial/forceful sense) and *said* are used to typify the boss's speech and *piped, quavered, peered* and *stared* are used to typify Woodifield's speech and actions. It is also possible to trace the events of the story through the verbs associated with the boss. The story moves from things being *said*, to *thought* and *groaned* and finally to *noticed, decided* and *lifted* (the body of the fly).

Stage 4

Once learners have reported back on their findings they can be asked to examine the characters in more depth.

First they can be given a concordance on *boy* and *boy's*. This provides sufficient information for them to be able to make generalizations about the relationship of the boy with his father and the significance of that relationship. It also gives the information needed in order to complete the next task.

```
                                      boy        8


MANS    32   h over the table of a grave-looking boy in uniform standing in one of those spe
MANS   108   h had opened up and he had seen the boy lying there with Woodifield's girls sta
MANS   111   away, the boss never thought of the boy except as lying unchanged, unblemished
MANS   119   ut not he. How was it possible? His boy was his only son. Ever since his birth
MANS   121   other meaning if it was not for the boy. Life itself had come to have no other
MANS   126   d been so near being fulfilled. The boy had been in the office learning the rop
MANS   132   d Macey couldn't make enough of the boy. And he wasn't in the least spoilt. No,
MANS   147    was cold, even stern- looking. The boy had never looked like that. At that mom


                                      boy's      5


MANS    72   d they happened to come across your boy's. They're quite near each other, it se
MANS   107   rang that remark upon him about the boy's grave. It had been exactly as though
MANS   114   rst months and even years after the boy's death, he had only to say those words
MANS   124   thout the promise before him of the boy's stepping into his shoes and carrying
MANS   130   gratulations he had received as the boy's father! No wonder; he had taken to it
```

Here concordances on the pronouns *his* and *him* are given. These can be particularly effective as material for discussion. The task is to decide which character is referred to by each instance of the pronoun (e.g. A = boss; B = boy; W = Woodifield; C = other). Learners have to justify their decisions and compare their findings with those of different groups.

```
                                     his     45

MANS     2   he great, green-leather armchair by his friend the boss's desk as a baby peers
MANS     3   sk as a baby peers out of its pram. His talk was over, it was time for him to
MANS     5    to go. Since he had retired, since his ... stroke, the wife and the girls kep
MANS     9   gine. Made a nuisance of himself to his friends, they supposed .... Well, perh
MANS    13   greedily at the boss, who rolled in his office chair, stout, rosy, five years
MANS    20   As a matter of fact he was proud of his room; he liked to have it admired, esp
MANS    37   tell you," said old Woodifield, and his eyes grew dim remembering. "Now what w
MANS    38   d when I started out this morning." His hands began to tremble, and patches of
MANS    39   le, and patches of red showed above his beard. Poor old chap, he's on his last
MANS    40   e his beard. Poor old chap, he's on his last pins, thought the boss. And, feel
MANS    44   't hurt a child." He took a key off his watch- chain, unlocked a cupboard belo
MANS    45   h- chain, unlocked a cupboard below his desk, and drew forth and dark, squat b
MANS    62   stuff like this. Ah!" He tossed off his, pulled out a handkerchief, hastily wi
MANS    62   d out a handkerchief, hastily wiped his moustaches, and cocked an eye at old W
MANS    64   oodifield, who was silently rolling his in his chaps. The old man swallowed, w
MANS    64   ld, who was silently rolling his in his chaps. The old man swallowed, was sile
MANS    67   !" But it warmed him; it crept into his chill old brain - he remembered. "That
MANS    69   t," he said, heaving himself out of his chair. "I thought you'd like to know.
MANS    74   oss made no reply. Only a quiver in his eyelids showed that he heard. The girl
MANS    81   ice broad paths." It was plain from his voice how much he liked a nice broad p
MANS    93   't the least idea. He came round by his desk, follow the shuffling footsteps t
MANS    97    watching him, dodged in and out of his cubby-hole like a dog that expects to
MANS   104   d leaning forward, the boss covered his face with his hands. He wanted, he int
MANS   104   ard, the boss covered his face with his hands. He wanted, he intended, he had
MANS   111    as lying unchanged, unblemished in his uniform, asleep for ever. "My son!" gr
MANS   119   n, but not he. How was it possible? His boy was his only son. Ever since his b
MANS   119   e. How was it possible? His boy was his only son. Ever since his birth the bos
MANS   119   is boy was his only son. Ever since his birth the boss had worked at building
MANS   124   fore him of the boy's stepping into his shoes and carrying on where he left of
MANS   131   had taken to it marvellously. As to his popularity with the staff, every man j
MANS   133   n the least spoilt. No, he was just his bright natural self, with the right wo
MANS   134    the right word for everybody, with his boyish look and his habit of saying ,
MANS   134   everybody, with his boyish look and his habit of saying , "Simply splendid.!"
MANS   138   ught the whole place crashing about his head. "Deeply regret to inform you ...
MANS   139   e had left the office a broken man, his life in ruins. Six years ago, six year
MANS   142   e happened yesterday. The boss took his hands from his face; he was puzzled. S
MANS   142   erday. The boss took his hands from his face; he was puzzled. Something seemed
MANS   146   it wasn't a favourite photograph of his; the expression was unnatural. It was
MANS   148    noticed that a fly had fallen into his broad ink pot, and was feebly but desp
MANS   165   en the boss had an idea. He plunged his pen back into the ink, leaned his thic
MANS   166   d his pen back into the ink, leaned his thick wrist on the blotting paper, and
MANS   177   nd the boss had just time to refill his pen, to shake fair and square on the n
MANS   191   Look sharp!" And he stirred it with his pen - in vain. Nothing happened or was
MANS   200   What was it? It was ... He took out his handkerchief and passed it inside his
MANS   201   s handkerchief and passed it inside his collar. For the life of him he could n
```

```
                                          him    18

MANS    4    His talk was over, it was time for him to be off. But he did not want to go.
MANS    5    stroke, the wife and the girls kept him boxed up in the house every day of the
MANS   15    at the helm. It did one good to see him. Wistfully, admiringly, the old man ad
MANS   21    pecially by old Woodifield. It gave him a feeling of deep, solid satisfaction
MANS   34    photographers' storm- clouds behind him. It was not new. It had been there for
MANS   52    rned the bottle and lovingly showed him the label. Whisky it was. "D'you know,
MANS   67    aintly, "It's nutty!" But it warmed him; it crept into his chill old brain - h
MANS   97    - haired office messenger, watching him, dodged in and out of his cubby-hole 1
MANS  106    ... It had been a terrible shock to him when old Woodifield sprang that remark
MANS  107     Woodifield sprang that remark upon him about the boy's grave. It had been exa
MANS  109     Woodifield's girls staring down at him. For it was strange. Although over six
MANS  116    iolent fit of weeping could relieve him. Time, he had declared then, he told e
MANS  120    ed at building up this business for him; it had no other meaning if it was not
MANS  124    se years without the promise before him of the boy's stepping into his shoes a
MANS  137     day had come when Macey had handed him the telegram that brought the whole pl
MANS  143    . Something seemed to be wrong with him. He wasn't feeling as he wanted to fee
MANS  195    ding feeling of wretchedness seized him that he felt positively frightened. He
```

Stage 5

The final stage for such a study might be a more conventional written (or spoken) report on the story or characters. Here the learners should be encouraged to draw on the insights they have gained from the concordance study. Questions like: *The boss seems to be a strong and successful person. Is this true?* will give learners the chance to use the information they have found out in class. If they are encouraged to support their arguments with close reference to the text of the story they should be able to incorporate their findings from the concordance-based activities.

c Comment

These types of activity provide a focus for discussion of a literary text. This is usually a new experience which learners find stimulating and exciting. Where groups have some experience of using this sort of evidence they can then be set investigative tasks – or, even better, decide on tasks for themselves. An excellent start for such studies is the word-frequency table. Once learners have access to information about the relative frequencies it is usually quite easy to decide on which words to investigate.

Through using the concordancer on a regular basis, learners begin to develop strategies for dealing with a wide variety of writing styles and texts. As a result of this kind of text analysis learners are able to use literature as a way of increasing their knowledge of English as well as to enjoy literature in English in its own right.

3 Teaching a short story: "Texts for Nothing, 1" by Samuel Beckett

In addition to providing valuable insights into such areas as characterization, a concordancer can also be used to isolate more subtle textual features. The second example in this chapter deals with a more unconventional piece of writing, the "Text for Nothing, 1" (1967).

a The text

This has none of the familiar features of plot and character of the Mansfield text. It has, however, been used successfully with non-specialist foreign language learners, who expressed surprise at how much they got out of the story and were keen to read more work of this type.

The piece is short (1,514 words), and very tightly structured. The reader has a sense of a movement through the story from some sort of unhappiness to some sort of reconciliation. The narrative voice is just that, a voice without a speaker. The voice talks to itself and we make of it what we can.

> "Suddenly, no, at last, long last, I couldn't any more, I couldn't go on. Someone said, You can't stay here. I couldn't stay there and I couldn't go on. I'll describe the place, that's unimportant." (p.72)

b A lesson

Stage 1: Preparation

The first thing that the concordancer was used for was to construct a wordlist. This is often a very good way of approaching a piece of writing when you are not sure how you want to use it in the classroom. The wordlist simply tells you about relative frequencies of occurrence, but it is surprising how much you can get out of this unsophisticated data (see overleaf).

Here the frequency of the definite article is unsurprising, but the frequency of the first person personal pronoun is extremely unusual. Having produced a wordlist, the next stage is to decide which of these items would actually be useful in a lesson.

Once you have an idea of which words occur in the text and of their relative frequencies, it is possible to select search strings and start hunting for patterns. In this case, as there was no obvious set of words that could be classed together, a concordance was done on all words with frequencies greater than 10. With such a short text this only takes a few minutes, but if you are working with a standard 8088/8086 IBM compatible PC, an extended, multi-word search can take a matter of hours when dealing with very large corpora.

the	88	can't	10	at	5
I	67	is	10	away	5
and	37	It's	10	can	5
to	36	same	10	come	5
it	34	so	10	day	5
in	29	up	9	down	5
All	26	I'm	8	eyes	5
my	26	more	8	had	5
me	23	not	8	I've	5
of	20	old	8	much	5
a	17	out	8	night	5
for	15	see	8	perhaps	5
what	14	that's	8	than	5
here	13	they	8	them	5
no	13	you	8	there	5
with	13	evening	7	will	5
go	12	from	7	an	4
was	12	stay	7	been	4
have	11	always	6	But	4
on	11	couldn't	6	by	4
one	11	again	5	certain	4
or	11	any	5	could	4
that	11	are	5	far	4
be	10	as	5	gone	4

The words that seemed the most interesting for teaching purposes were not at all obvious. They were:

all (26) *here* (13) *in* (29) *me* (23) *my* (26) *so* (10)

The concordance for *in* is given opposite.

Simply reading through this set of samples is an amazingly effective way of giving a representative cross-section of the text. It is possible to trace a shift of mood that begins with the bleakness of lines 7, 11 and 15, and continues through the *hammered lead, glacial loughs, down in the hole, face in the dark, as in a graveyard* of lines 29 to 36. There is a transition at *breathing in and out* in line 63, the mid-point of the story. From here onwards there is a move towards a more more reconciled and harmonious mood. Clustered around *in* one now finds: *My rheumatism it hurts in any case, Eye ravening patient in the haggard vulture face, toiling up the slope* which is eventually followed by: *hand in hand, sunk in our worlds, I'm in my arms, I'm holding myself in my arms, without much tenderness, but faithfu* ... . The effect created by this type of concordance is to produce a kind of cross-section of the text, which is much more useful for students to discuss than the whole story.

```
  7  ooped deep by the rains. It was far down  in one of these I was lying, out of the wind
 11  ssessed you to come? I could have stayed  in my den, snug and dry, I couldn't. My den,
 15  t struggling, like an old hack foundered  in the street, struggling no more , struggli
 29   heard tell of the view, the distant sea  in hammered lead, the so-called golden vale
 31  le valleys, the glacial loughs, the city  in its haze, it was all on every tongue. Who
 33  e, go before me, come with me? I am down  in the hole the centuries have dug, centurie
 34  uries of filthy weather, flat on my face  in the dark earth sodden with the creeping s
 36  inks. They are up above, all round me as  in a graveyard, I can't raise my eyes to the
 38   their faces, their legs perhaps plunged  in the heath. Do they see me, what can they
 41   I mean the same as ever, strange. think  in the valley the sun is blazing all down th
 63  hat I'm doing , all-important, breathing  in and out and saying , with words like smok
 66  mself alright, only muffled, like buried  in snow, less the warmth, less the drowse, I
 69  ast I presume so, I'm far. My rheumatism  in any case is no more than a memory, , it h
 70  ase is no more than a memory, , it hurts  in any case is no more than a memory, It hur
 71  , when it hurt her. Eye ravening patient  in the haggard vulture face, perhaps it's ca
 76   another. One thing at least is certain,  in an hour it will be too late, in half-an-h
 77  certain, in an hour it will be too late,  in half-an-hour it will be night, and yet it
 87  't be here yet, toiling up the slope, or  in the bracken by the wood, it's larch, I do
 99  like breathing your last to put new life  in you, and then the rooms, natural death, t
100  then the rooms, natural death, tucked up  in bed, smothered in household gods, and alw
100  tural death, tucked up in bed, smothered  in household gods, and always muttering, the
102  ame old questions and answers, no malice  in me, hardly any, stultior stultissimo, nev
109  r children, , it all happened on a rock,  in the storm, the mother was dead and the gu
118  n't believe, or we walked together, hand  in hand, silent, sunk in our worlds, each in
119  ked together, hand in hand, silent, sunk  in our worlds, each in his world, the hands
119  n hand, silent, sunk in our worlds, each  in his world, the hands forgotten in each ot
119  , each in his world, the hands forgotten  in each other. That's how I've held out till
121  vening again it seems to be working, I'm  in my arms, I'm holding myself in my arms, w
122  king, I'm in my arms, I'm holding myself  in my arms, without much tenderness, but fai
```

Stage 2: Organizing the lesson

This story was given to a group of general English students in the year that they were preparing to take the Cambridge Proficiency Examination. One of them was a literature student, but the others came from a wide variety of backgrounds and, although they had chosen a Literature option, they had no specialist interest in this sort of writing.

The class members were not asked to read the text before the class, but in previous classes they had studied Graham Greene's story "The Invisible Chinese Gentleman" and Muriel Spark's "The House of the Famous Poet" (both in Malcom Bradbury, *Modern British Short Stories*, Penguin, 1988). In these classes discussion had centred on narrative structure and authorial intervention, and the whole idea of "play" in language. The Beckett story was chosen because it seemed a good example of a text that slips further from conventional models of well-constructed narrative than these other stories, yet is dense and rigorously constructed.

As a pre-reading task the students were asked to see if they could identify any structure to the story during their first reading.

As the story is a single, uninterrupted paragraph this presents quite a challenge. The sorts of comments ranged from: "The sentences get longer as you go through..." to "There's somebody talking to himself and as he remembers a story he starts to feel happier ...", but the students found it difficult to say much more initially. They were able to recognize the problem that the first person *I* presented and one student mentioned the difficulty of the following sentence, which comes towards the end of the story:

> "Yes, I was my father and I was my son, I asked myself questions and answered as best I could, I had it told to me evening after evening, the same old story I knew by heart and couldn't believe, or we walked together, hand in hand, silent, sunk in our worlds, each in his world, the hands forgotten in each other."

This moves away from "reliable" narrative of the type which they had studied in the Muriel Spark story.

At this point the class was divided into groups and given different concordance printouts. One group had *all* and *me.* another *in* and *here* and a third *my* and *so.* Their first task was to see if they could find a shape to the story more easily now that they had a more manageable cross-section to deal with. They were asked to do this by marking where they felt there were important transitions in the story. Their second task was to see if they could retell the story as a third person account. They were asked to say what "somebody" was doing in this story, just using the information from the concordances.

This was surprisingly effective. Each group was able to give a version of the text. All of these versions had a common structure, even though they responded to different aspects of wording in the text. All of the groups were able to identify a beginning, a middle, and an end to the story on the basis of the concordance they were studying, and were able to come up with an effective retelling.

At this stage of the lesson, all of the students were asked to study the *in* concordance and see if they could describe the narrative progression through the story. They were also asked to suggest which aspects of the text might have caused the responses that the class had registered on initial reading. This second investigative phase brought up many of the points discussed in Stage 1 above. It was particularly interesting to note that it was quite often the non-specialists who came up with the most telling observations. Not being obliged to be "sensitive" they were very happy to talk about what was simply under their noses.

The students then nominated a spokesperson for each group who reported back to the class. Disagreements were discussed and points which the class agreed on were noted down.

Using concordancing software with this "difficult" text made it possible for students with no specialist literary background to get to grips with the sort of writing that would normally be considered too obscure. The learners were able to see how narrative structure was maintained in spite of the apparent absence of conventional narration, and they were able to arrive at a reading of the story that was independent of any ideas of plot, character or theme.

4 Other applications

This chapter has given just a very brief glimpse of some of the ways in which the concordancer can help students use literature in their language courses. Whether it will be possible to extend the use of text-handling software in literature teaching will depend on how much time teachers have to type texts into the computer, and on how many literary documents are available in machine-readable form. Nevertheless, it is certain that this approach gives students an opportunity to begin to read literature in the second language at a level that would probably be unattainable otherwise. As teachers collect more and more samples for analysis, and as students become more confident in their ability to deal with these "slippery" documents, there is enormous scope for exciting work in this area. The application of concordancing and other text-handling tools to the teaching of drama and poetry, the study of different styles of writing through the analysis of short extracts and the comparison of literatures from World English will make the language classroom an even more creative and exciting place.

Chapter summary

- Concordancing software can be very useful when dealing with short, individual texts such as short stories and poems.

- Wordlists can be an effective first step in studying short texts.

- You can use concordances to do conventional studies of plot, theme or character and also use them when working on "difficult" texts.

- If you are able to accumulate large collections of literary writing it becomes possible to use the concordancer to do comparative studies for such areas as style.

7

Do-it-yourself Concordances

1 WordPerfect 5

Printed below is a simple, interactive KWIC concordancer written using WordPerfect version 5.0 macros. The concordancer can work with ASCII files (it strips out all unnecessary hard returns in the results) or with WP5 documents.

The concordancer asks the user to set an appropriate font for document 2 where the concordance will be printed, (this makes it possible to both print and display the text as a series of unbroken, 120-character lines). It then asks for an exact keyword or phrase (surrounded by spaces in order to avoid getting parts of words). An "end of concordance + word-count" message is temporarily displayed at the bottom of document 1 and the results are shown in the second document.

```
{DISPLAY OFF}
{ASSIGN}1 0                                    {;}sets a counter
{Switch}
{Format}170{Enter}0{Enter}{Enter}{Enter}    {;}formats document two
{DISPLAY ON}
{PROMPT}Select a condensed font after this message.
(press RETURN to continue)
{PAUSE}
{Font}4{Macro Commands}1{Enter}{Enter}       {;}set font
{DISPLAY OFF}
{Switch}
{DISPLAY ON}                                   {;}call for input
{TEXT}2 Type in the exact word or phrase you want to study:
{DISPLAY OFF}
{LABEL}start {Search}{VAR 2}{Search}     {;}starts the search
{ASSIGN}1 {VAR 1}+1                       {;}updates the counter
{ON NOT FOUND}{GO}report                 {;}specifies action on fail
{Word Left}                              {;}define & copy a block
{Left}{Left}{Left}{Left}{Left}{Left}{Left}{Left}{Left}{Left}{Left}
{Left}{Left}{Left}{Left}{Left}{Left}{Left}{Left}{Left}{Left}{Left}
```

```
{Left}{Left}{Left}{Left}{Left}{Left}{Left}{Left}{Left}{Left}
{Left}{Left}{Left}{Left}{Left}{Left}{Left}{Left}{Left}{Left}
{Left}{Left}{Left}{Left}{Left}{Left}{Left}{Left}{Left}{Left}
{Left}{Left}{Left}{Left}{Left}
{Block}
{Right}{Right}{Right}{Right}{Right}{Right}{Right}{Right}{Right}
{Right}{Right}{Right}{Right}{Right}{Right}{Right}{Right}{Right}
{Right}{Right}{Right}{Right}{Right}{Right}{Right}{Right}{Right}
{Right}{Right}{Right}{Right}{Right}{Right}{Right}{Right}{Right}
{Right}{Right}{Right}{Right}{Right}{Right}{Right}{Right}{Right}
{Right}{Right}{Right}{Right}{Right}{Right}{Right}{Right}{Right}
{Right}{Right}{Right}{Right}{Right}{Right}{Right}{Right}{Right}
{Right}{Right}{Right}{Right}{Right}{Right}{Right}{Right}{Right}
{Right}{Right}{Right}{Right}{Right}{Right}{Right}{Right}{Right}
{Right}{Right}{Right}{Right}{Right}{Right}{Right}{Right}{Right}
{Right}{Right}{Right}{Right}{Right}{Right}{Right}{Right}{Right}
{Right}{Right}{Right}{Right}{Right}{Right}{Right}{Right}{Right}
{Right}{Right}{Right}
{Move}12{Switch}{Enter}
{CALL}strip                          {;}strips hard returns
{Home}{Home}{Home}{Down}{Enter}
{Switch}
{Left}{Left}{Left}{Left}{Left}{Left}{Left}{Left}{Left}{Left}
{Left}{Left}{Left}{Left}{Left}{Left}{Left}{Left}{Left}{Left}
{Left}{Left}{Left}{Left}{Left}{Left}{Left}{Left}{Left}{Left}
{Left}{Left}{Left}{Left}{Left}{Left}{Left}{Left}{Left}{Left}
{Left}{Left}{Left}{Left}{Left}{Left}{Left}{Left}{Left}{Left}
{Left}{Left}{Left}{Left}{Left}
{Word Right}{GO}start            {;}loop the macro
{LABEL}strip                     {;}function to strip hard returns
{Replace}n{Enter}{Search} {Search}
{ON NOT FOUND}{RETURN}
{RETURN}
{LABEL}report                    {;}final format function
{DISPLAY ON}
{PROMPT}"{VAR 2}" occurs {VAR 1} times.  To view the concordance
press [RETURN]
{PAUSE}
{DISPLAY OFF}                     {;}sets header and label text
{Switch}
{Home}{Home}{Up}{Enter}{Up}{Esc}60{Enter}{Esc} {VAR 2}    ({VAR 1})
{Enter}{Home}{Home}{Down}{Enter}
{Bold}Concordance results for "{VAR 2}"{Bold}{Block}{Word Left}
{Switch}1{End}
```

The macro contains explicit comment lines and it is easy to reproduce using the built in WordPerfect 5 macro editor. Refer to your manual if you have not used the editor before and be sure to copy the above text exactly. Pay particular attention to the tilde [~] character which has to be given twice [~~] in some contexts. All command functions (e.g. {ASSIGN}) are obtained by using Ctrl+PageUp and then selecting from the Commands menu. Run the macro by using Ctrl+F10 and then naming it (e.g. CONCO).

2 Basic programming algorithm – Concordancing in BASIC

If you enjoy programming in BASIC you may like to try writing your own concordancer. There is little point in giving an example program here as dialects of BASIC vary so much. They are particularly variable in the way in which they read data from disc files and in the maximum permissible size of strings. Both of these features have a considerable bearing on the best way to approach writing a program.

Figures 1 and 2 show an algorithm which should be easy to implement in any BASIC (such as BBC BASIC) which allows you to read data from an ASCII file one byte at a time keeping track of the file pointer. The algorithm is simple but slow, as it involves reading in every word of the text and comparing it with the keyword. It should be possible to speed it up by adapting it to read whole chunks of text into long strings and then using an INSTR function to search for the keyword. Exactly how you do this will depend, again, on the BASIC that you use. In the form given it should be quite fast enough to cope with short documents.

Figure 1 gives the overall structure of the program in its simplest possible form. Figure 2 shows the flowchart of the "guts" of the program, the module "SEARCH", which could be written as a subroutine or procedure.

FIGURE 1

```
Get input filename

Get output filename

Get keyword (=KEYWORD$)

Open files

SEARCH (see Figure 2)

Close files
```

FIGURE 2

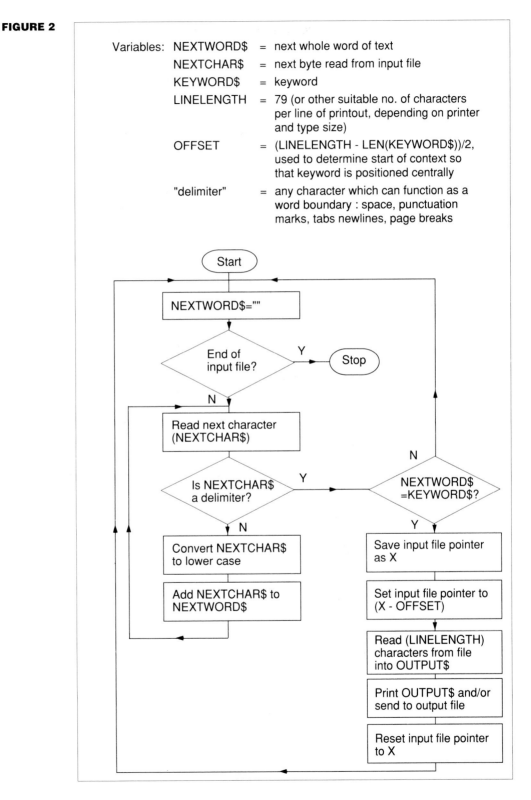

Variables: NEXTWORD$ = next whole word of text
            NEXTCHAR$ = next byte read from input file
            KEYWORD$ = keyword
            LINELENGTH = 79 (or other suitable no. of characters
                         per line of printout, depending on printer
                         and type size)
            OFFSET   = (LINELENGTH - LEN(KEYWORD$))/2,
                         used to determine start of context so
                         that keyword is positioned centrally
            "delimiter" = any character which can function as a
                         word boundary : space, punctuation
                         marks, tabs newlines, page breaks

3 WORD4

The following is a macro which will work with Microsoft WORD version 4.0 (and upwards). It operates on one text (the current WORD document) at a time. Its effect is to create a second window containing the concordance output. This can then be viewed on screen, printed, edited or saved as separate document. The way in which the macro works is explained in the «COMMENT» statements within the macro text. These can be omitted, of course, when you copy the macro into your WORD glossary.

«COMMENT»

```
Concordancing Macro
for Microsoft WORD (ver 4.0 upwards)
```

Source text should be loaded before this macro is invoked. KWIC output is sent to a second window. From here it can be printed or saved as a separate file.

VARIABLES:

occ = number of occurrences
file = filename of source text
keyword = keyword
whole = flag to set search for whole word (y) or part word

«ENDCOMMENT»

«SET occ=0»

«COMMENT get name of source file»
<esc>ts
«SET file=field»<esc>

«COMMENT get keyword»
«ASK keyword=?Enter keyword and press ↵ »
«ASK whole=?Whole word (y/n + ↵)»

«COMMENT open second window»
<esc>w<enter><enter>6<tab>y<enter>

«COMMENT strip out tabs, paragraphs, newlines and page» «COMMENT breaks and replace with temporary dummy»
«COMMENT characters»
<f1><ctrl pgup>
<esc>r^^t<tab>τ <tab><space><tab 2>n<enter>
<esc>r^^p<tab>^T<tab><space><enter>
<esc>r^^n<tab>η <tab><space><enter>
<esc>r^^d<tab>^U<tab><space><enter>
```
```

«COMMENT add dummy string to end of text to prevent»
«COMMENT looping if keyword in last 35 characters»
<ctrl pgdn>
XXXXXXXXXXXXXXXXXXXXXXXXXXXXXXXX

«COMMENT start search»
<ctrl pgup>
<esc>s«keyword»<tab 3>«whole»<enter>

«IF NOTFOUND»
«MESSAGE Keyword not found»
<esc>wc2<enter>n
«QUIT»
«ENDIF»

«COMMENT select line of text and»
«COMMENT copy to lower window»
«SET occ=occ+1»
<left 35><f6><right 79><del><ins><left 35>

Concordance of «keyword» in «file»:<enter><enter>
<ins><enter>

«COMMENT continue search»
«WHILE FOUND»
<f1><shift f4>

«IF NOTFOUND»

«COMMENT reinstate page breaks etc and delete XXXs»
<ctrl pgup>
<esc>rτ<tab>^^t<tab><space><tab 2>n<enter>
<esc>r^T<tab>^^p<tab><space><enter>
<esc>rη<tab>^^n<tab><space><enter>
<esc>r^U<tab>^^d<tab><space><enter>
<ctrl pgdn><f7><del>
<f1><enter><enter>«occ» occurrences

«COMMENT set margins in window 2 to full page»
<esc>fdm<tab 2>0<tab>0<enter>
«QUIT»
«ENDIF»

«COMMENT select line of text and»
«COMMENT copy to lower window»
«SET occ=occ+1»
<left 35><f6><right 79><del><ins><left 35>
<f1><ins><enter>
«ENDWHILE»

Appendix – Organisations and journals

MUESLI (Micro Users in ESL Institutions)

the computer users' Special Interest Group of IATEFL (the International Association of Teachers of English as a Foreign Language)

MUESLI publishes a newsletter, *MUESLI News*, four or five times a year, and holds meetings in the UK, and occasionally elsewhere in Europe, at similar intervals. At MUESLI meetings there is usually time set aside for the exchange of ideas, software and text files.

IATEFL, 3 Kingsdown Champers, Kingsdown Park, Tankerton, Whitstable, Kent, CT5 2DJ, United Kingdom

ICAME (International Computer Archive of Modern English)

publishes a newsletter, *ICAME News*, and is probably the best source of information on supplies of public domain and research corpora.

Norwegian Computing Centre for the Humanities, P.O. Box 53, Bergen, Norway

TESOL (Teachers of English to Speakers of Other Languages)

has a CALL Interest Section which publishes *CALL Interest Section Newsletter*.

Suite 205, 1118 22nd Street, N.W., Washington, DC 20037, USA

EUROCALL (European Computer Assisted Language Learning Group)

is a group of CALL practitioners, mostly based in universities, in various European countries. EUROCALL holds meetings and conferences at irregular intervals and publishes a newsletter called *RECALL*.

EUROCALL, Institute of English Language Education, Bailrigg, Lancaster University, Lancaster, LA1 4YT, United Kingdom

Other journals

CAELL Journal (International Society for Technology in Education)

four issues per year, each devoted to a particular theme in Computer Assisted Language Learning.

University of Oregon, 1787 Agate Street, Eugene, OR 97403, USA

SYSTEM (International Journal of Educational Technology and Language Learning Systems)

a quarterly journal containing scholarly articles on all aspects of Language Teaching, especially applications of recent technology.

Pergamon Press, Headington Hill Hall, Oxford, OX3 0BW, United Kingdom

CALL (Computer Assisted Language Learning)

three issues per year.

Intellect Books, Suite 2, 108/110 London Road, Oxford, OX3 9AW, United Kingdom

Software bibliography

This brief "bibliography" covers both concordancing software and word processing software that is currently available and which the authors know to have good concordancing potential. It does not pretend to be exhaustive and does not cover software which is either unpublished or was unavailable to us prior to going to press.

Framework

Ashton-Tate Corporation, Maidenhead, UK

See the article by Joseph Rézeau in the bibliography for information on the potential of Framework.

Longman Mini-Concordancer

Longman Group UK Ltd, Harlow, Essex, CM20 2JE, UK

A powerful, in-memory text-handling program with excellent text information, wildcard, sort, wordlist and search facilities. It allows the user to window back to the original full context of any KWIC concordance line, but is limited to texts of around 50,000 words when used with a PC compatible computer with 640Kb memory. LMC does not need a hard disk to run. This concordancing package has very significant classroom potential as a result of its easy-to-use interface and the tremendous speed with which it generates and sorts wordlists and concordances. At the time of writing it is the only software of which we are aware that can be thoroughly recommended for classroom use, as well for a wide range of non-teaching applications.

Micro OCP

Oxford University Computing Service, Oxford University Press,
Walton Street, Oxford, OX2 6DP, UK

At present (1989), OCP is the most comprehensive dedicated concordancing program available for the PC. It provides text processing facilities for files of unlimited length (dependent on the size of your hard disk) and excellent post-processing text format features. Developed from a mainframe program, Micro OCP is not easy to use or quick. This makes it more suitable as an academic research tool or for materials preparation than a real option for classroom research. Its slowness can make it very frustrating when you are working with even medium sized text files (300Kb +).

Microsoft WORD 4

Microsoft Limited, Excel House, 49 De Montfort Road, Reading, RG1 8LP, UK

Microsoft WORD 4 (and indeed WORD 5) has very powerful programmable macros that enable the user to repeat a range of keystrokes and construct concordances formatted as lines, sentences or words. It also has the considerable advantage of making available a true "word" definition for macro searches.

WordCruncher

Electronic Text Corporation. 56000, North University Avenue, Provo, Utah, UT 84604, USA

WordCruncher is an extremely sophisticated program. It is, in reality, two sets of software; an INDEX program which constructs wordlists and a fully indexed version of your original document (which can be in WordPerfect format or ASCII – file length is purely a function of available hard disk space); and a VIEW program which gives you various options for viewing the information contained in your indexed documents. When you wish to study a text file you can access sentence contexts for any word, phrases or word combinations and window back into the original full text context. If you take advantage of the text labelling facilities in the INDEX program you are also able to get detailed information on the exact location of each example. WordCruncher can also generate detailed concordances for words or phrases which contain full source information.

The great advantage of WordCruncher is that the only time-consuming process involved in its use is text indexing. Once this has been done all VIEW operations can be carried out with considerable speed and ease. A drawback in its design is that it is not possible to see the concordances you have generated without exiting from the program and going into a word-processor.

WordPerfect 5.0

WordPerfect UK, Wellington House, New Zealand Avenue, Walton-on-Thames, Surrey, KTY 1PY, UK

Very powerful and easily edited macros give WordPerfect 5 considerable potential for concordancing. Although not so quick or flexible as a dedicated program, if you have a hard disk, this is one of the most effective tools for materials preparation and is ideal for editing concordances produced by other programs.

Bibliography

Bongarts T *et al*, 1988 *Computer Applications in Language Learning*, Foris

Johns T, 1986 *Micro-Concord, a Language Learner's Research Tool*, System, 14(2): p.151–162

Johns T, 1988 *Whence and whither classroom concordancing?* in Bongarts T *et al*, 1988 Computer Applications in Language Learning, Foris

Jones R L, 1988 *WordCruncher in the language classroom: computer assisted text analysis and computer-aided instruction*, Foreign Language, March/April 1988

Garside R, Leech G, & Sampson G, 1987 *The Computational Analysis of English: a corpus-based approach*, Longman, Harlow

Hardisty W & Windeatt S, 1989 *CALL*, in the series Resource Books for Teachers, Oxford University Press

Phillips M, 1987 *Microcomputers and the teaching of literature*, Literary and Linguistic Computing 2 (3), 1987

Rézeau J, 1988 *De l'utilisation d'un progiciel professionel en E.A.O. des langues: ou comment FRAMEWORK est devenu FRAMETEACH*, Le Français dans le Monde, Aug/September 1988

Sinclair J M, 1987 *Looking up: An account of the COBUILD Project in lexical computing*, Collins, London

Tribble C T, 1988, *The use of text structuring vocabulary in native and non-native speaker writing*, MUESLI News (Micro Users in ESL Institutions), June 1989

Windeatt S, 1987 *Concordances in Language Teaching, RECALL Computers in English Language and Research*, 3 (February) 1987